THE NEW FOLGER LIBRARY SHAKESPEARE

Designed to make Shakespeare's great plays available to all readers, the New Folger Library edition of Shakespeare's plays provides accurate texts in modern spelling and punctuation, as well as scene-by-scene action summaries, full explanatory notes, many pictures clarifying Shakespeare's language, and notes recording all significant departures from the early printed versions. Each play is prefaced by a brief introduction, by a guide to reading Shakespeare's language, and by accounts of his life and theater. Each play is followed by an annotated list of further readings and by a "Modern Perspective" written by an expert on that particular play.

Barbara A. Mowat is Director of Academic Programs at the Folger Shakespeare Library, Executive Editor of *Shakespeare Quarterly,* Chair of the Folger Institute, and author of *The Dramaturgy of Shakespeare's Romances* and of essays on Shakespeare's plays and on the editing of the plays.

Paul Werstine is Professor of English at the Graduate School and at King's University College at the University of Western Ontario. He is general editor of the New Variorum Shakespeare and author of many papers and articles on the printing and editing of Shakespeare's plays.

The Folger Shakespeare Library

The Folger Shakespeare Library in Washington, D.C., a privately funded research library dedicated to Shakespeare and the civilization of early modern Europe, was founded in 1932 by Henry Clay and Emily Jordan Folger. In addition to its role as the world's preeminent Shakespeare collection and its emergence as a leading center for Renaissance studies, the Folger Library offers a wide array of cultural and educational programs and services for the general public.

EDITORS

BARBARA A. MOWAT
Director of Academic Programs
Folger Shakespeare Library

PAUL WERSTINE
Professor of English
King's University College at the University of
Western Ontario, Canada

FOLGER SHAKESPEARE LIBRARY

Much Ado About Nothing

By
WILLIAM SHAKESPEARE

EDITED BY BARBARA A. MOWAT
AND PAUL WERSTINE

Simon & Schuster Paperbacks
NEW YORK   LONDON   TORONTO   SYDNEY

Simon & Schuster Paperbacks
A Division of Simon & Schuster, Inc.
1230 Avenue of the Americas
New York, NY 10020

First Washington Square Press New Folger Trade Paperback Edition August 2005
This Simon & Schuster paperback edition February 2009

SIMON & SCHUSTER PAPERBACKS and colophon are registered trademarks of Simon & Schuster, Inc.

For information regarding special discounts for bulk purchases, please contact Simon & Schuster Special Sales at 1-866-506-1949 or business@simonandschuster.com.

The Simon & Schuster Speakers Bureau can bring authors to your live event. For more information or to book an event, contact the Simon & Schuster Speakers Bureau at 1-866-248-3049 or visit our website at www.simonspeakers.com.

Manufactured in the United States of America

10 9 8 7 6 5 4

ISBN-13: 978-0-7434-8494-7
ISBN-10:   0-7434-8494-0

From the Director of the Library

For over four decades, the Folger Library General Reader's Shakespeare provided accurate and accessible texts of the plays and poems to students, teachers, and millions of other interested readers. Today, in an age often impatient with the past, the passion for Shakespeare continues to grow. No author speaks more powerfully to the human condition, in all its variety, than this actor/playwright from a minor sixteenth-century English village.

Over the years vast changes have occurred in the way Shakespeare's works are edited, performed, studied, and taught. The New Folger Library Shakespeare replaces the earlier versions, bringing to bear the best and most current thinking concerning both the texts and their interpretation. Here is an edition which makes the plays and poems fully understandable for modern readers using uncompromising scholarship. Professors Barbara Mowat and Paul Werstine are uniquely qualified to produce this New Folger Shakespeare for a new generation of readers. The Library is grateful for the learning, clarity, and imagination they have brought to this ambitious project.

Werner Gundersheimer,
Director of the Folger Shakespeare Library
from 1984 to 2002

Contents

Editors' Preface

In recent years, ways of dealing with Shakespeare's texts and with the interpretation of his plays have been undergoing significant change. This edition, while retaining many of the features that have always made the Folger Shakespeare so attractive to the general reader, at the same time reflects these current ways of thinking about Shakespeare. For example, modern readers, actors, and teachers have become interested in the differences between, on the one hand, the early forms in which Shakespeare's plays were first published and, on the other hand, the forms in which editors through the centuries have presented them. In response to this interest, we have based our edition on what we consider the best early printed version of a particular play (explaining our rationale in a section called "An Introduction to This Text") and have marked our changes in the text—unobtrusively, we hope, but in such a way that the curious reader can be aware that a change has been made and can consult the "Textual Notes" to discover what appeared in the early printed version.

Current ways of looking at the plays are reflected in our brief prefaces, in many of the commentary notes, in the annotated lists of "Further Reading," and especially in each play's "Modern Perspective," an essay written by an outstanding scholar who brings to the reader his or her fresh assessment of the play in the light of today's interests and concerns.

As in the Folger Library General Reader's Shakespeare, which this edition replaces, we include explanatory notes designed to help make Shakespeare's language clearer to a modern reader, and we place the notes on the page facing the text that they explain. We also follow the earlier edition in including illustrations —of objects, of clothing, of mythological figures—from books and manuscripts in the Folger Library collection. We provide fresh accounts of the life of Shakespeare, of the publishing of his plays, and of the theaters in which his plays were performed, as well as an introduction to the text itself. We also include a section called "Reading Shakespeare's Language," in which we try to help readers learn to "break the code" of Elizabethan poetic language.

For each section of each volume, we are indebted to a host of generous experts and fellow scholars. The "Reading Shakespeare's Language" sections, for example, could not have been written had not Arthur King, of Brigham Young University, and Randal Robinson, author of *Unlocking Shakespeare's Language,* led the way in untangling Shakespearean language puzzles and generously shared their insights and methodologies with us. "Shakespeare's Life" profited by the careful reading given it by S. Schoenbaum, "Shakespeare's Theater" was read and strengthened by Andrew Gurr and John Astington, and "The Publication of Shakespeare's Plays" is indebted to the comments of Peter W. M. Blayney. We, as editors, take sole responsibility for any errors in our editions.

We are grateful to the authors of the "Modern Perspectives"; to Leeds Barroll and David Bevington for their generous encouragement; to the Huntington and Newberry Libraries for fellowship support; to King's College for the grants it has provided to Paul Werstine; to the Social Sciences and Humanities Research Council of Canada, which provided him with a Research Time Stipend for 1990–91; to R. J. Shroyer of the University of Western Ontario for essential computer support; to Penny Gill and Eva Mary Hooker for insightful conversations about the language of *Much Ado About Nothing;* to Skiles Howard and Scott Reiss for advice on Renaissance music and dance; and to the Folger Institute's Center for Shakespeare Studies for its fortuitous sponsorship of a workshop on "Shakespeare's Texts for Students and Teachers" (funded by the National Endowment for the Humanities and led by Richard Knowles of the University of Wisconsin), a workshop from which we learned an enormous amount about what is wanted by college and high-school teachers of Shakespeare today.

Our biggest debt is to the Folger Shakespeare Library —to Werner Gundersheimer, Director of the Library, who made possible our edition; to Jean Miller, the Library's Art Curator, who combs the Library holdings for illustrations, and to Julie Ainsworth, Head of the Photography Department, who carefully photographs them; to Peggy O'Brien, Director of Education, and her assistant, Molly Haws, who continue to give us expert advice about the needs being expressed by Shakespeare teachers and students (and to Martha Christian and other "master teachers" who used our texts in manuscript in their classrooms); to Jessica Hymowitz, who provides expert computer support; to the staff of the Academic Programs Division, especially Mary Tonkinson, Lena Cowen Orlin, Toni Krieger, Amy Adler, Kathleen Lynch, and Carol Brobeck; and, finally, to the staff of the Library Reading Room, whose patience and support are invaluable.

Barbara A. Mowat and Paul Werstine

Shakespeare's
Much Ado About Nothing

Much Ado About Nothing is one of Shakespeare's more popular comedies, with a long history of success on the stage. Much of its appeal lies in its two stories of romantic love with their quite different journeys to comedy's happy ending. Hero and Claudio fall in love almost at first sight; their union has the blessing of the older generation (in the persons of Hero's father, Leonato, and Claudio's prince, Don Pedro). All should be well. But from the outside comes the virulent force of Don John, who acts with the kind of malice that strikes out at whatever promises to make someone else happy. For Hero and Claudio to find happiness, they must go beyond Don John's treachery, Claudio's own weak jealousy, Don Pedro's touchy sense of his own honor, and Leonato's too credulous paternal fury. It takes a second (unlikely) outside force in the guise of the bumbling, officious Dogberry to offer any hope of bringing Hero's truth to light.

The story of Beatrice and Benedick is quite other. They are kept apart not by a vicious outsider but by their pride in their own brilliance and by their mutual antagonism and distrust. Both express aversion to marriage; each finds particular pleasure in attacking the other. To outsiders, they seem an ideal pair. So the outsiders decide to play Cupid.

Over the centuries the Beatrice-Benedick plot has most captivated audiences and readers. King Charles I, in his copy of Shakespeare's plays, crossed out the play's title and renamed it "Beatrice and Benedick," and a prefatory poem in a 1640 edition of Shakespeare's sonnets says, "Let but *Beatrice* / And *Benedick* be seene,

Map of Spain, France, and Italy.

From Giovanni Botero, *Le relationi vniuersali* . . . (1618).

lo, in a trice / The Cockpit, Galleries, Boxes all are full."
And Berlioz's opera version of *Much Ado* is named
Béatrice et Bénédict. It is generally agreed that Beatrice
and Benedick are the model for the witty lovers in comic
drama of later centuries; and it can be argued that they
led as well to Jane Austen's Elizabeth and Darcy in *Pride
and Prejudice* and to Scarlett and Rhett in *Gone With the
Wind.*

It is, however, the conjunction of the Beatrice and
Benedick story with the story of Hero and Claudio that
makes *Much Ado* so rich and rewarding a play. Beatrice
and Benedick, faced with humiliating descriptions of
what they had considered their most prized character
traits, learn to "suffer love" and to "eat their meat
without grudging"; simultaneously, Claudio and Hero
are forced into an experience that acquaints them first
with life's darkness (with treachery, betrayal, vicious
jealousy, public shaming, and abandonment) and then
with quite unexpected joy (with the recovery of the
irrevocably lost, with discovery at the unlikely hands of
the play's "shallow fools"). It can be argued that, while
the play calls itself "Much Ado About *Nothing,*" its stories
are actually much ado about life at its most important.

After you have read the play, we invite you to turn to
the back of this book and read *"Much Ado About Nothing:
A Modern Perspective,"* by Professor Gail Kern Paster of
George Washington University.

Reading Shakespeare's Language: *Much Ado About Nothing*

For many people today, reading Shakespeare's language
can be a problem—but it is a problem that can be

solved. Those who have studied Latin (or even French or German or Spanish), and those who are used to reading poetry, will have little difficulty understanding the language of Shakespeare's poetic drama. Others, though, need to develop the skills of untangling unusual sentence structures and of recognizing and understanding poetic compressions, omissions, and wordplay. And even those skilled in reading unusual sentence structures may have occasional trouble with Shakespeare's words. Four hundred years of "static" intervene between his speaking and our hearing. Most of his immense vocabulary is still in use, but a few of his words are not, and, worse, some of his words now have meanings quite different from those they had in the sixteenth century. In the theater, most of these difficulties are solved for us by actors who study the language and articulate it for us so that the essential meaning is heard—or, when combined with stage action, is at least *felt*. When reading on one's own, one must do what each actor does: go over the lines (often with a dictionary close at hand) until the puzzles are solved and the lines yield up their poetry and the characters speak in words and phrases that are, suddenly, rewarding and wonderfully memorable.

Shakespeare's Words

As you begin to read the opening scenes of a play by Shakespeare, you may notice occasional unfamiliar words. Some are unfamiliar simply because we no longer use them. In the opening scenes of *Much Ado About Nothing*, for example, you will find the words *squarer* (i.e., fighter, quarreler), *methinks* (it seems to me), *recheat* (the notes of a hunting horn), *baldrick* (a belt for holding bugles, swords, etc.), and *arras* (a hanging

Palazzo regio

Arsenale

Torre mozza

Gigno città di Calabria

Torre di pendinole

Messina.

From Pietro Bertelli, *Theatrum vrbium Italicarum* . . . (1599).

screen of rich tapestry fabric). Words of this kind are explained in notes to the text and will become familiar the more of Shakespeare's plays you read.

In *Much Ado About Nothing*, as in all of Shakespeare's writing, more problematic are the words that we still use but that we use with a different meaning. In the opening scenes of *Much Ado*, for example, the word *tax* has the meaning of "take to task, criticize," *stomach* is used where we would say "appetite," *halting* where we would say "limping," *sad* where we would say "serious," and *winded* where we would say "sounded, blown." Such words will be explained in the notes to the text, but they, too, will become familiar as you continue to read Shakespeare's language.

Some words are strange not because of the "static" introduced by changes in language over the past centuries but because these are words that Shakespeare is using to build a dramatic world that has its own geography and history and background mythology. *Much Ado About Nothing*, for example, through references to Messina, Venice, and Padua, to "thick-pleached alleys" and "orchards," creates a location on a wealthy estate in Italy. Through military language—*action* (i.e., military engagement), *sort* (i.e., rank), and *sworn brother* (i.e., brother-in-arms)—it places itself in time, just at the end of a war. Through complicated references to Cupid and his arrows and to Hercules (a mythological figure prominent both for his massive strength and for his helplessness when trapped by love), it also builds a world in which warfare and romantic love are intricately intertwined. These "local" words and references (each of which will be explained in notes to this text) help to build the world that Beatrice, Benedick, Hero, and Claudio inhabit, and will become increasingly familiar to you as you read further into the play.

Shakespearean Wordplay

In *Much Ado About Nothing,* Shakespeare plays with language so often and so variously that the entire play can be read and heard as brilliant repartee: witty punning, elaboration of commonplaces, highly figured verbal structures. In the play's opening scene, the Messenger delivers his report of the just-ended war in elaborate verbal figures. He reports that Claudio "hath borne himself beyond the promise of his age, doing in the figure of a lamb the feats of a lion," thus contrasting Claudio's lamblike youth and apparent helplessness with his lionlike ferocity in battle. He then uses figured language to report Claudio's uncle's reception of the news of Claudio's valor: "there appears much joy in him, even so much that joy could not show itself modest enough without a badge of bitterness." (*Badge* here means "sign" and *bitterness* means "anguish of heart, suffering.") These words are such a complicated way of saying "He was so happy he wept" that Leonato is forced to ask for clarification: "Did he break out into tears?" The Messenger's response, "In great measure," leads in turn to Leonato's punning response: "A kind overflow of kindness," where *kind* means both "natural" and "warmhearted" and *kindness* means both "kinship" and "affection."

Every major character in *Much Ado About Nothing* has his or her own way of playing with, elaborating, or misusing language. Two of the more intriguing are Beatrice and Benedick, whose linguistic tendencies define them for the other characters. Beatrice, in the prejudice of the time, is seen as "shrewish" or "curst" because of her "sharp tongue." Her first line in the play is to ask whether "Signior Mountanto" (i.e., Benedick) has returned from the war, jabbing at Benedick by naming him with the fencing term *montant* (an upward blow or thrust). More typical of her wordplay is her response to the Messenger's "I see, lady, the gentleman is not in your books." The Messenger is, of course, using the phrase "in your books" figuratively, to mean "in your favor"; she takes the phrase literally and replies "No. An [i.e., if] he were, I would burn my study [i.e., library]." A few lines earlier we find her again taking a figurative phrase and interpreting it literally: when the Messenger describes Benedick as a man "stuffed with all honorable virtues," she responds "It is so indeed. He is no less than a stuffed man, but for the stuffing—well, we are all mortal." In the fourth scene of the play, when her uncle says to her "Well, niece, I hope to see you one day fitted with a husband," she builds an elaborate response by taking literally the more-or-less figurative biblical passage which reads that "the Lord God formed man of the dust of the ground" (Genesis 2:7). Combining a literal reading of this verse with the line in the marriage liturgy in which the woman promises to "obey" and "serve" the man she marries, Beatrice responds as follows to Leonato's wish that she find a husband: "Not till God make men of some other metal than earth. Would it not grieve a woman to be overmastered with a piece of valiant dust? To make an account of her life to a clod of wayward marl?" It is to such language that the male characters in the play respond: "By my troth . . . , thou wilt never get thee a husband if thou be so shrewd of thy tongue."

Benedick, too, uses wordplay centered in the double meanings of words (saying, for example, that Hero is "too low for a high praise, too brown for a fair praise, and too little for a great praise"). But his more characteristic wordplay is with metaphor—or, rather, with metaphoric figures. A true metaphor is a play on words in which one object or idea is expressed as if it were something else, something with which it shares common features. (Don John uses metaphor when he says "I have decreed not to sing in my cage," picturing his unfree state as that of a caged songbird.) Benedick's metaphoric figures begin as metaphors or similes but spin out into linguistic cartoons: "Prove that ever I lose more blood with love than I will get again with drinking," he boasts, "pick out mine eyes with a ballad-maker's pen and hang me up at the door of a brothel house for the sign of blind Cupid." With a few phrases, he sketches himself as first blinded, then turned into a signboard, and then hung outside a brothel. "If I [fall in love]," he again boasts, "hang me in a bottle like a cat and shoot at me, and he that hits me, let him be clapped on the shoulder and called Adam." Here the wordplay is built on a simile (i.e., he is to be *like* a cat in a bottle), but again the comparison image expands into an entire scenario in which Benedick is to be hung in a bottle, used for archery practice, hit by an arrow, and the winner congratulated. One of his metaphoric overstatements comes back to haunt him. Answering Don Pedro's quoting of the proverb "In time the savage bull doth bear the yoke," Benedick comically dooms himself by saying "The savage bull may, but if ever the sensible Benedick bear it, pluck off the bull's horns and set them in my forehead, and let me be vilely painted, and in such great letters as they write 'Here is good horse to hire' let them signify under my sign 'Here you may see Benedick the married man.'" The image produced here—the sensible Benedick wearing the bull's horns and advertising his married state—seems to be a challenge to Don Pedro that is later picked up in his tricking of Benedick and that is alluded to twice toward the end of the play. One of the play's high comic moments rests on Benedick's turning Claudio's taunts about the savage bull back on Claudio, using metaphoric language to shape a truly elegant riposte:

PRINCE
   Good morrow, Benedick. Why, what's the matter
   That you have such a February face,
   So full of frost, of storm, and cloudiness?
CLAUDIO
   I think he thinks upon the savage bull.
   Tush, fear not, man. We'll tip thy horns with gold,
   And all Europa shall rejoice at thee,
   As once Europa did at lusty Jove
   When he would play the noble beast in love.
BENEDICK
   Bull Jove, sir, had an amiable low,
   And some such strange bull leapt your father's cow
   And got a calf in that same noble feat
   Much like to you, for you have just his bleat.
                                        (5.4.41–52)

Benedick's metaphoric conversational style is what leads Don Pedro to characterize Benedick as being "from the crown of his head to the sole of his foot . . . all mirth" (3.2.8–9). This style is also, no doubt, what lies behind Beatrice's taunting characterization of him as "the Prince's jester" (2.1.135).

Because intricate wordplay—whether the intentional elaborations of Benedick and Beatrice or the unintentional confusions of Dogberry—is so central to the language structure of *Much Ado About Nothing*, one must read the dialogue with special attention to double meanings, elaborated metaphors, verbal confusions, and other forms of linguistic playfulness.

Implied Stage Action

In reading Shakespeare's plays we must always remember that what we are reading is a performance script. The dialogue is written to be spoken by actors who, at the same time, are moving, gesturing, picking up objects, weeping, shaking their fists. Some stage action is described in what are called "stage directions"; some is suggested within the dialogue itself. We must learn to be alert to such signals as we stage the play in our imaginations. When, in *Much Ado About Nothing* 2.3, Benedick says "I will hide me in the arbor," and a few lines later Don Pedro says "See you where Benedick hath hid himself?" it is clear that the stage action involves Benedick's hiding behind a stage tree (or some structure onstage that represents part of an "arbor"). Again, in 3.1, the stage action is mapped out rather precisely in Hero's line "For look where Beatrice like a lapwing runs / Close by the ground," followed by Ursula's "Beatrice . . . even now / Is couchèd in the woodbine coverture," and Hero's "Then go we near her, that her ear lose nothing / Of the false sweet bait that we lay for it."

At several places in *Much Ado About Nothing*, signals to the reader are not quite so clear. Early in the first wedding scene, Claudio, having been "given" Hero, gives her back again to her father with the lines "There, Leonato, take her back again. / Give not this rotten orange to your friend." It is unclear just what Claudio's actions are as he delivers those lines. In many productions, he throws her toward Leonato, sometimes with such violence that she hits the stage in a bruised heap. One could argue that, since this is early in the scene's action, before Claudio's rage truly builds, a less violent gesture is more appropriate, but a range of stage actions offers itself. Again, later in the same scene, Beatrice's question "Why, how now, cousin, wherefore sink you down?" makes it clear that Hero falls to the stage. When she should get back up, however, is left to the imagination of the director, the actress, or us as readers to determine. Learning to read the language of stage action repays one many times over when one reads the play's final scene, with its entrance of masked ladies, its powerful unmasking of the "Hero that is dead," its discovery of the love letters that demonstrate that Beatrice and Benedick do, in fact, love each other, and its final dance. Here, as in so much of *Much Ado About Nothing,* implied stage action vitally affects our response to the play.

It is immensely rewarding to work carefully with Shakespeare's language so that the words, the sentences, the wordplay, and the implied stage action all become clear—as readers for the past four centuries have discovered. It may be more pleasurable to attend a good performance of a play—though not everyone has thought so. But the joy of being able to stage one of Shakespeare's plays in one's imagination, to return to passages that continue to yield further meanings (or further questions) the more one reads them—these are pleasures that, for many, rival (or at least augment) those of the performed text, and certainly make it worth considerable effort to "break the code" of Elizabethan poetic drama and let free the remarkable language that makes up a Shakespeare text.

Shakespeare's Life

Surviving documents that give us glimpses into the life of William Shakespeare show us a playwright, poet, and actor who grew up in the market town of Stratford-upon-Avon, spent his professional life in London, and returned to Stratford a wealthy landowner. He was born in April 1564, died in April 1616, and is buried inside the chancel of Holy Trinity Church in Stratford.

We wish we could know more about the life of the world's greatest dramatist. His plays and poems testify to his wide reading—especially to his knowledge of Virgil, Ovid, Plutarch, Holinshed's *Chronicles,* and the Bible—and to his mastery of the English language, but we can only speculate about his education. We know that the King's New School in Stratford-upon-Avon was considered excellent. The school was one of the English "grammar schools" established to educate young men, primarily in Latin grammar and literature. As in other schools of the time, students began their studies at the age of four or five in the attached "petty school," and there learned to read and write in English, studying primarily the catechism from the Book of Common Prayer. After two years in the petty school, students entered the lower form (grade) of the grammar school, where they began the serious study of Latin grammar and Latin texts that would occupy most of the remainder of their school days. (Several Latin texts that Shakespeare used repeatedly in writing his plays and poems were texts that schoolboys memorized and recited.) Latin comedies were introduced early in the lower form; in the upper form, which the boys entered at age ten or eleven, students wrote their own Latin orations and declamations, studied Latin historians and rhetoricians, and began the study of Greek using the Greek New Testament.

Since the records of the Stratford "grammar school" do not survive, we cannot prove that William Shakespeare attended the school; however, every indication (his father's position as an alderman and bailiff of

CATECHISMVS

paruus pueris primùm Latinè
qui ediscatur, proponendus
in Scholis.

LONDINI
Apud Iohannem Dayum Typo-
graphum. An. 1573.

Cum Priuilegio Regiæ Maieſtatis.

A catechism.
Title page of *Catechismvs paruus pueris primum Latine . . .* (1573).

Stratford, the playwright's own knowledge of the Latin classics, scenes in the plays that recall grammar-school experiences—for example, *The Merry Wives of Windsor*, 4.1) suggests that he did. We also lack generally accepted documentation about Shakespeare's life after his schooling ended and his professional life in London began. His marriage in 1582 (at age eighteen) to Anne Hathaway and the subsequent births of his daughter Susanna (1583) and the twins Judith and Hamnet (1585) are recorded, but how he supported himself and where he lived are not known. Nor do we know when and why he left Stratford for the London theatrical world, nor how he rose to be the important figure in that world that he had become by the early 1590s.

We do know that by 1592 he had achieved some prominence in London as both an actor and a playwright. In that year was published a book by the playwright Robert Greene attacking an actor who had the audacity to write blank-verse drama and who was "in his own conceit [i.e., opinion] the only Shake-scene in a country." Since Greene's attack includes a parody of a line from one of Shakespeare's early plays, there is little doubt that it is Shakespeare to whom he refers, a "Shake-scene" who had aroused Greene's fury by successfully competing with university-educated dramatists like Greene himself. It was in 1593 that Shakespeare became a published poet. In that year he published his long narrative poem *Venus and Adonis;* in 1594, he followed it with *The Rape of Lucrece*. Both poems were dedicated to the young earl of Southampton (Henry Wriothesley), who may have become Shakespeare's patron.

It seems no coincidence that Shakespeare wrote these narrative poems at a time when the theaters were closed because of the plague, a contagious epidemic disease that devastated the population of London. When

The Globe

A stylized representation of the Globe theater.
From Claes Jansz Visscher, *Londinum Florentissima
Britanniae Urbs* . . . (c. 1625).

the theaters reopened in 1594, Shakespeare apparently resumed his double career of actor and playwright and began his long (and seemingly profitable) service as an acting-company shareholder. Records for December of 1594 show him to be a leading member of the Lord Chamberlain's Men. It was this company of actors, later named the King's Men, for whom he would be a principal actor, dramatist, and shareholder for the rest of his career.

So far as we can tell, that career spanned about twenty years. In the 1590s, he wrote his plays on English history as well as several comedies and at least two tragedies (*Titus Andronicus* and *Romeo and Juliet*). These histories, comedies, and tragedies are the plays credited to him in 1598 in a work, *Palladis Tamia*, that in one chapter compares English writers with "Greek, Latin, and Italian Poets." There the author, Francis Meres, claims that Shakespeare is comparable to the Latin dramatists Seneca for tragedy and Plautus for comedy, and calls him "the most excellent in both kinds for the stage." He also names him "Mellifluous and honey-tongued Shakespeare": "I say," writes Meres, "that the Muses would speak with Shakespeare's fine filed phrase, if they would speak English." Since Meres also mentions Shakespeare's "sugared sonnets among his private friends," it is assumed that many of Shakespeare's sonnets (not published until 1609) were also written in the 1590s.

In 1599, Shakespeare's company built a theater for themselves across the river from London, naming it the Globe. The plays that are considered by many to be Shakespeare's major tragedies (*Hamlet, Othello, King Lear,* and *Macbeth*) were written while the company was resident in this theater, as were such comedies as *Twelfth Night* and *Measure for Measure.* Many of Shakespeare's plays were performed at court (both for

Queen Elizabeth I and, after her death in 1603, for King James I), some were presented at the Inns of Court (the residences of London's legal societies), and some were doubtless performed in other towns, at the universities, and at great houses when the King's Men went on tour; otherwise, his plays from 1599 to 1608 were, so far as we know, performed only at the Globe. Between 1608 and 1612, Shakespeare wrote several plays—among them *The Winter's Tale* and *The Tempest*—presumably for the company's new indoor Blackfriars theater, though the plays seem to have been performed also at the Globe and at court. Surviving documents describe a performance of *The Winter's Tale* in 1611 at the Globe, for example, and performances of *The Tempest* in 1611 and 1613 at the royal palace of Whitehall.

Shakespeare wrote very little after 1612, the year in which he probably wrote *King Henry VIII*. (It was at a performance of *Henry VIII* in 1613 that the Globe caught fire and burned to the ground.) Sometime between 1610 and 1613 he seems to have returned to live in Stratford-upon-Avon, where he owned a large house and considerable property, and where his wife and his two daughters and their husbands lived. (His son Hamnet had died in 1596). During his professional years in London, Shakespeare had presumably derived income from the acting company's profits as well as from his own career as an actor, from the sale of his play manuscripts to the acting company, and, after 1599, from his shares as an owner of the Globe. It was presumably that income, carefully invested in land and other property, which made him the wealthy man that surviving documents show him to have become. It is also assumed that William Shakespeare's growing wealth and reputation played some part in inclining the crown, in 1596, to grant John Shakespeare, William's father, the coat of arms that he had so long sought. William Shakespeare died in Stratford on April 23, 1616 (according to the epitaph carved under his bust in Holy Trinity Church) and was buried on April 25. Seven years after his death, his collected plays were published as *Mr. William Shakespeares Comedies, Histories, & Tragedies* (the work now known as the First Folio).

The years in which Shakespeare wrote were among the most exciting in English history. Intellectually, the discovery, translation, and printing of Greek and Roman classics were making available a set of works and worldviews that interacted complexly with Christian texts and beliefs. The result was a questioning, a vital intellectual ferment, that provided energy for the period's amazing dramatic and literary output and that fed directly into Shakespeare's plays. The Ghost in *Hamlet*, for example, is wonderfully complicated in part because he is a figure from Roman tragedy—the spirit of the dead returning to seek revenge—who at the same time inhabits a Christian hell (or purgatory); Hamlet's description of humankind reflects at one moment the Neoplatonic wonderment at mankind ("What a piece of work is a man!") and, at the next, the Christian disparagement of human sinners ("And yet, to me, what is this quintessence of dust?").

As intellectual horizons expanded, so also did geographical and cosmological horizons. New worlds—both North and South America—were explored, and in them were found human beings who lived and worshiped in ways radically different from those of Renaissance Europeans and Englishmen. The universe during these years also seemed to shift and expand. Copernicus had earlier theorized that the earth was not the center of the cosmos but revolved as a planet around the sun. Galileo's telescope, created in 1609, allowed scientists to see that Copernicus had been correct; the universe was not organized with the earth at the center, nor was it so nicely circumscribed as people had, until that time, thought. In terms of expanding horizons, the impact of these discoveries on people's beliefs—religious, scientific, and philosophical—cannot be overstated.

London, too, rapidly expanded and changed during the years (from the early 1590s to around 1610) that Shakespeare lived there. London—the center of England's government, its economy, its royal court, its overseas trade—was, during these years, becoming an exciting metropolis, drawing to it thousands of new citizens every year. Troubled by overcrowding, by poverty, by recurring epidemics of the plague, London was also a mecca for the wealthy and the aristocratic, and for those who sought advancement at court, or power in government or finance or trade. One hears in Shakespeare's plays the voices of London—the struggles for power, the fear of venereal disease, the language of buying and selling. One hears as well the voices of Stratford-upon-Avon—references to the nearby Forest of Arden; to sheep herding, to small-town gossip, to village fairs and markets. Part of the richness of Shakespeare's work is the influence felt there of the various worlds in which he lived: the world of metropolitan London, the world of small-town and rural England, the world of the theater, and the worlds of craftsmen and shepherds.

That Shakespeare inhabited such worlds we know from surviving London and Stratford documents, as well as from the evidence of the plays and poems themselves. From such records we can sketch the dramatist's life. We know from his works that he was a voracious reader. We know from legal and business documents that he was a multifaceted theater man who became a wealthy landowner. We know a bit about his family life and a fair amount about his legal and financial dealings. Most scholars today depend upon such evidence as they draw their picture of the world's greatest playwright. Such, however, has not always been the case. Until the late eighteenth century, the William Shakespeare who lived in most biographies was the creation of legend and tradition. This was the Shakespeare who was supposedly caught poaching deer at Charlecote, the estate of Sir Thomas Lucy close by Stratford; this was the Shakespeare who fled from Sir Thomas's vengeance and made his way in London by taking care of horses outside a playhouse; this was the Shakespeare who reportedly could barely read but whose natural gifts were extraordinary, whose father was a butcher who allowed his gifted son sometimes to help in the butcher shop, where William supposedly killed calves "in a high style," making a speech for the occasion. It was this legendary William Shakespeare whose Falstaff (in *1* and *2 Henry IV*) so pleased Queen Elizabeth that she demanded a play about Falstaff in love, and demanded that it be written in fourteen days (hence the existence of *The Merry Wives of Windsor*). It was this legendary Shakespeare who reached the top of his acting career in the roles of the Ghost in *Hamlet* and old Adam in *As You Like It*—and who died of a fever contracted by drinking too hard at "a merry meeting" with the poets Michael Drayton and Ben Jonson. This legendary Shakespeare is a rambunctious, undisciplined man, as attractively "wild" as his plays were seen by earlier generations to be. Unfortunately, there is no trace of evidence to support these wonderful stories.

Perhaps in response to the disreputable Shakespeare of legend—or perhaps in response to the fragmentary and, for some, all-too-ordinary Shakespeare documented by surviving records—some people since the mid-nineteenth century have argued that William Shakespeare could not have written the plays that bear his name. These persons have put forward some dozen names as more likely authors, among them Queen Elizabeth I, Sir Francis Bacon, Edward de Vere (earl of Oxford), and Christopher Marlowe. Such attempts to find what for these people is a more believable author of the plays is a tribute to the regard in which the plays are held. Unfortunately for their claims, the documents that exist that provide evidence for the facts of Shakespeare's life tie him inextricably to the body of plays and poems that bear his name. Unlikely as it seems to those who want the works to have been written by an aristocrat, a university graduate, or an "important" person, the plays and poems seem clearly to have been produced by a man from Stratford-upon-Avon with a very good "grammar-school" education and a life of experience in London and in the world of the London theater. How this particular man produced the works that dominate the cultures of much of the world almost four hundred years after his death is one of life's mysteries—and one that will continue to tease our imaginations as we continue to delight in his plays and poems.

Shakespeare's Theater

The actors of Shakespeare's time are known to have performed plays in a great variety of locations. They played at court (that is, in the great halls of such royal residences as Whitehall, Hampton Court, and Greenwich); they played in halls at the universities of Oxford and Cambridge, and at the Inns of Court (the residences in London of the legal societies); and they also played in the private houses of great lords and civic officials. Sometimes acting companies went on tour from London into the provinces, often (but not only) when outbreaks of bubonic plague in the capital forced the closing of theaters to reduce the possibility of contagion in crowded audiences. In the provinces the actors usually staged their plays in churches (until around 1600) or in guildhalls. While surviving records show only a handful of occasions when actors played at inns while on tour, London inns were important playing places up until the 1590s.

The building of theaters in London had begun only shortly before Shakespeare wrote his first plays in the 1590s. These theaters were of two kinds: outdoor or public playhouses that could accommodate large numbers of playgoers, and indoor or private theaters for much smaller audiences. What is usually regarded as the first London outdoor public playhouse was called simply the Theatre. James Burbage—the father of Richard Burbage, who was perhaps the most famous actor in Shakespeare's company—built it in 1576 in an area north of the city of London called Shoreditch. Among the more famous of the other public playhouses that capitalized on the new fashion were the Curtain and the Fortune (both also built north of the city), the Rose, the Swan, the Globe, and the Hope (all located on the Bankside, a region just across the Thames south of the city of London). All these playhouses had to be built outside the jurisdiction of the city of London because many civic officials were hostile to the performance of drama and repeatedly petitioned the royal council to abolish it.

The theaters erected on the Bankside (a region under the authority of the Church of England, whose head was the monarch) shared the neighborhood with houses of prostitution and with the Paris Garden, where the blood sports of bearbaiting and bullbaiting were carried on. There may have been no clear distinction between playhouses and buildings for such sports, for we know that the Hope was used for both plays and baiting and that Philip Henslowe, owner of the Rose and, later, partner in the ownership of the Fortune, was also a partner in a monopoly on baiting. All these forms of entertainment were easily accessible to Londoners by boat across the Thames or over London Bridge.

Evidently Shakespeare's company prospered on the Bankside. They moved there in 1599. Threatened by difficulties in renewing the lease on the land where their first theater (the Theatre) had been built, Shakespeare's company took advantage of the Christmas holiday in 1598 to dismantle the Theatre and transport its timbers across the Thames to the Bankside, where, in 1599, these timbers were used in the building of the Globe. The weather in late December 1598 is recorded as having been especially harsh. It was so cold that the Thames was "nigh [nearly] frozen," and there was heavy snow. Perhaps the weather aided Shakespeare's company in eluding their landlord, the snow hiding their activity and the freezing of the Thames allowing them to slide the timbers across to the Bankside without paying tolls for repeated trips over London Bridge. Attractive as this narrative is, it remains just as likely that the heavy snow hampered transport of the timbers in wagons through the London streets to the river. It also must be remembered that the Thames was, according to report, only "nigh frozen" and therefore as impassable as it ever was. Whatever the precise circumstances of this fascinating event in English theater history, Shakespeare's company was able to begin playing at their new Globe theater on the Bankside in 1599. After the first Globe burned down in 1613 during the staging of Shake-speare's *Henry VIII* (its thatch roof was set alight by cannon fire called for by the performance), Shake-speare's company immediately rebuilt on the same location. The second Globe seems to have been a grander structure than its predecessor. It remained in use until the beginning of the English Civil War in 1642, when Parliament officially closed the theaters. Soon thereafter it was pulled down.

The public theaters of Shakespeare's time were very different buildings from our theaters today. First of all, they were open-air playhouses. As recent excavations of the Rose and the Globe confirm, some were polygonal or roughly circular in shape; the Fortune, however, was square. The most recent estimates of their size put the diameter of these buildings at 72 feet (the Rose) to 100 feet (the Globe), but we know that they held vast audiences of two or three thousand, who must have been squeezed together quite tightly. Some of these spectators paid extra to sit or stand in the two or three levels of roofed galleries that extended, on the upper levels, all the way around the theater and surrounded an open space. In this space were the stage and, perhaps, the tiring house (what we would call dressing rooms), as well as the so-called yard. In the yard stood the specta-tors who chose to pay less, the ones whom Hamlet contemptuously called "groundlings." For a roof they had only the sky, and so they were exposed to all kinds of weather. They stood on a floor that was sometimes made of mortar and sometimes of ash mixed with the shells of hazelnuts. The latter provided a porous and therefore dry footing for the crowd, and the shells may have been more comfortable to stand on because they were not as hard as mortar. Availability of shells may not have been a problem if hazelnuts were a favorite food for Shake-

speare's audiences to munch on as they watched his
plays. Archaeologists who are today unearthing the
remains of theaters from this period have discovered
quantities of these nutshells on theater sites.

Unlike the yard, the stage itself was covered by a roof.
Its ceiling, called "the heavens," is thought to have been
elaborately painted to depict the sun, moon, stars, and
planets. Just how big the stage was remains hard to
determine. We have a single sketch of part of the interior
of the Swan. A Dutchman named Johannes de Witt
visited this theater around 1596 and sent a sketch of it
back to his friend, Arend van Buchel. Because van
Buchel found de Witt's letter and sketch of interest, he
copied both into a book. It is van Buchel's copy,
adapted, it seems, to the shape and size of the page in his
book, that survives. In this sketch, the stage appears to
be a large rectangular platform that thrusts far out into
the yard, perhaps even as far as the center of the circle
formed by the surrounding galleries. This drawing,
combined with the specifications for the size of the stage
in the building contract for the Fortune, has led scholars
to conjecture that the stage on which Shakespeare's
plays were performed must have measured approxi-
mately 43 feet in width and 27 feet in depth, a vast acting
area. But the digging up of a large part of the Rose by
archaeologists has provided evidence of a quite different
stage design. The Rose stage was a platform tapered at
the corners and much shallower than what seems to be
depicted in the van Buchel sketch. Indeed, its measure-
ments seem to be about 37.5 feet across at its widest
point and only 15.5 feet deep. Because the surviving
indications of stage size and design differ from each
other so much, it is possible that the stages in other
theaters, like the Theatre, the Curtain, and the Globe
(the outdoor playhouses where we know that Shake-

speare's plays were performed), were different from those at both the Swan and the Rose.

After about 1608 Shakespeare's plays were staged not only at the Globe but also at an indoor or private playhouse in Blackfriars. This theater had been constructed in 1596 by James Burbage in an upper hall of a former Dominican priory or monastic house. Although Henry VIII had dissolved all English monasteries in the 1530s (shortly after he had founded the Church of England), the area remained under church, rather than hostile civic, control. The hall that Burbage had purchased and renovated was a large one in which Parliament had once met. In the private theater that he constructed, the stage, lit by candles, was built across the narrow end of the hall, with boxes flanking it. The rest of the hall offered seating room only. Because there was no provision for standing room, the largest audience it could hold was less than a thousand, or about a quarter of what the Globe could accommodate. Admission to Blackfriars was correspondingly more expensive. Instead of a penny to stand in the yard at the Globe, it cost a minimum of sixpence to get into Blackfriars. The best seats at the Globe (in the Lords' Room in the gallery above and behind the stage) cost sixpence; but the boxes flanking the stage at Blackfriars were half a crown, or five times sixpence. Some spectators who were particularly interested in displaying themselves paid even more to sit on stools on the Blackfriars stage.

Whether in the outdoor or indoor playhouses, the stages of Shakespeare's time were different from ours. They were not separated from the audience by the dropping of a curtain between acts and scenes. Therefore the playwrights of the time had to find other ways of signaling to the audience that one scene (to be imagined as occurring in one location at a given time) had ended and the next (to be imagined at perhaps a different location at a later time) had begun. The customary way used by Shakespeare and many of his contemporaries was to have everyone onstage exit at the end of one scene and have one or more different characters enter to begin the next. In a few cases, where characters remain onstage from one scene to another, the dialogue or stage action makes the change of location clear, and the characters are generally to be imagined as having moved from one place to another. For example, in *Romeo and Juliet,* Romeo and his friends remain onstage in Act 1 from scene 4 to scene 5, but they are represented as having moved between scenes from the street that leads to Capulet's house into Capulet's house itself. The new location is signaled in part by the appearance onstage of Capulet's servingmen carrying napkins, something they would not take into the streets. Playwrights had to be quite resourceful in the use of hand properties, like the napkin, or in the use of dialogue to specify where the action was taking place in their plays because, in contrast to most of today's theaters, the playhouses of Shakespeare's time did not use movable scenery to dress the stage and make the setting precise. As another consequence of this difference, however, the playwrights of Shakespeare's time did not have to specify exactly where the action of their plays was set when they did not choose to do so, and much of the action of their plays is tied to no specific place.

Usually Shakespeare's stage is referred to as a "bare stage," to distinguish it from the stages of the last two or three centuries with their elaborate sets. But the stage in Shakespeare's time was not completely bare. Philip Henslowe, owner of the Rose, lists in his inventory of stage properties a rock, three tombs, and two mossy banks. Stage directions in plays of the time also call for such things as thrones (or "states"), banquets (presumably tables with plaster replicas of food on them), and beds and tombs to be pushed onto the stage. Thus the stage often held more than the actors.

The actors did not limit their performing to the stage alone. Occasionally they went beneath the stage, as the Ghost appears to do in the first act of *Hamlet*. From there they could emerge onto the stage through a trapdoor. They could retire behind the hangings across the back of the stage (or the front of the tiring house), as, for example, the actor playing Polonius does when he hides behind the arras. Sometimes the hangings could be drawn back during a performance to "discover" one or more actors behind them. When performance required that an actor appear "above," as when Juliet is imagined to stand at the window of her chamber in the famous and misnamed "balcony scene," then the actor probably climbed the stairs to the gallery over the back of the stage and temporarily shared it with some of the spectators. The stage was also provided with ropes and winches so that actors could descend from, and reascend to, the "heavens."

Perhaps the greatest difference between dramatic performances in Shakespeare's time and ours was that in Shakespeare's England the roles of women were played by boys. (Some of these boys grew up to take male roles in their maturity.) There were no women in the acting companies, only in the audience. It had not always been so in the history of the English stage. There are records of women on English stages in the thirteenth and fourteenth centuries, two hundred years before Shakespeare's plays were performed. After the accession of James I in 1603, the queen of England and her ladies took part in entertainments at court called masques, and with the reopening of the theaters in 1660 at the restoration of Charles II, women again took their place on the public stage.

The chief competitors for the companies of adult actors such as the one to which Shakespeare belonged and for which he wrote were companies of exclusively boy actors. The competition was most intense in the early 1600s. There were then two principal children's companies: the Children of Paul's (the choirboys from St. Paul's Cathedral, whose private playhouse was near the cathedral); and the Children of the Chapel Royal (the choirboys from the monarch's private chapel, who performed at the Blackfriars theater built by Burbage in 1596, which Shakespeare's company had been stopped from using by local residents who objected to crowds). In *Hamlet* Shakespeare writes of "an aerie [nest] of children, little eyases [hawks], that cry out on the top of question and are most tyrannically clapped for 't. These are now the fashion and . . . berattle the common stages [attack the public theaters]." In the long run, the adult actors prevailed. The Children of Paul's dissolved around 1606. By about 1608 the Children of the Chapel Royal had been forced to stop playing at the Blackfriars theater, which was then taken over by the King's Men, Shakespeare's own troupe.

Acting companies and theaters of Shakespeare's time were organized in different ways. For example, Philip Henslowe owned the Rose and leased it to companies of actors, who paid him from their takings. Henslowe would act as manager of these companies, initially paying playwrights for their plays and buying properties, recovering his outlay from the actors. Shakespeare's company, however, managed itself, with the principal actors, Shakespeare among them, having the status of "sharers" and the right to a share in the takings, as well as the responsibility for a part of the expenses. Five of the sharers themselves, Shakespeare among them, owned the Globe. As actor, as sharer in an acting company and in ownership of theaters, and as playwright, Shakespeare was about as involved in the theatrical industry as one could imagine. Although Shakespeare and his fellows prospered, their status under the law was conditional upon the protection of powerful patrons. "Common players"—those who did not have patrons or masters—were classed in the language of the law with "vagabonds and sturdy beggars." So the actors had to secure for themselves the official rank of servants of patrons. Among the patrons under whose protection Shakespeare's company worked were the lord chamberlain and, after the accession of King James in 1603, the king himself.

We are now perhaps on the verge of learning a great deal more about the theaters in which Shakespeare and his contemporaries performed—or at least of opening up new questions about them. Already about 70 percent of the Rose has been excavated, as has about 10 percent of the second Globe, the one built in 1614. It is to be hoped that soon more will be available for study. These are exciting times for students of Shakespeare's stage.

The Publication of Shakespeare's Plays

Eighteen of Shakespeare's plays found their way into print during the playwright's lifetime, but there is nothing to suggest that he took any interest in their publication. These eighteen appeared separately in editions called quartos. Their pages were not much larger than

the one you are now reading, and these little books were
sold unbound for a few pence. The earliest of the
quartos that still survive were printed in 1594, the year
that both *Titus Andronicus* and a version of the play now
called *2 King Henry VI* became available. While almost
every one of these early quartos displays on its title page
the name of the acting company that performed the
play, only about half provide the name of the playwright,
Shakespeare. The first quarto edition to bear the name
Shakespeare on its title page is *Love's Labor's Lost* of
1598. A few of these quartos were popular with the
book-buying public of Shakespeare's lifetime; for example, quarto *Richard II* went through five editions between 1597 and 1615. But most of the quartos were far
from best-sellers; *Love's Labor's Lost* (1598), for instance, was not reprinted in quarto until 1631. After
Shakespeare's death, two more of his plays appeared in
quarto format: *Othello* in 1622 and *The Two Noble
Kinsmen*, coauthored with John Fletcher, in 1634.

In 1623, seven years after Shakespeare's death, *Mr.
William Shakespeares Comedies, Histories, & Tragedies*
was published. This printing offered readers in a single
book thirty-six of the thirty-eight plays now thought to
have been written by Shakespeare, including eighteen
that had never been printed before. And it offered them
in a style that was then reserved for serious literature
and scholarship. The plays were arranged in double
columns on pages nearly a foot high. This large page size
is called "folio," as opposed to the smaller "quarto,"
and the 1623 volume is usually called the Shakespeare
First Folio. It is reputed to have sold for the lordly price
of a pound. (One copy at the Folger Library is marked
fifteen shillings—that is, three-quarters of a pound.)

In a preface to the First Folio entitled "To the great
Variety of Readers," two of Shakespeare's former fellow

actors in the King's Men, John Heminge and Henry Condell, wrote that they themselves had collected their dead companion's plays. They suggested that they had seen his own papers: "we have scarce received from him a blot in his papers." The title page of the Folio declared that the plays within it had been printed "according to the True Original Copies." Comparing the Folio to the quartos, Heminge and Condell disparaged the quartos, advising their readers that "before you were abused with divers stolen and surreptitious copies, maimed, and deformed by the frauds and stealths of injurious impostors." Many Shakespeareans of the eighteenth and nineteenth centuries believed Heminge and Condell and regarded the Folio plays as superior to anything in the quartos.

Once we begin to examine the Folio plays in detail, it becomes less easy to take at face value the word of Heminge and Condell about the superiority of the Folio texts. For example, of the first nine plays in the Folio (one quarter of the entire collection), four were essentially reprinted from earlier quarto printings that Heminge and Condell had disparaged; and four have now been identified as printed from copies written in the hand of a professional scribe of the 1620s named Ralph Crane; the ninth, *The Comedy of Errors,* was apparently also printed from a manuscript, but one whose origin cannot be readily identified. Evidently then, eight of the first nine plays in the First Folio were not printed, in spite of what the Folio title page announces, "according to the True Original Copies," or Shakespeare's own papers, and the source of the ninth is unknown. Since today's editors have been forced to treat Heminge and Condell's pronouncements with skepticism, they must choose whether to base their own editions upon quartos or the Folio on grounds other than Heminge and Condell's story of where the quarto and Folio versions originated.

Editors have often fashioned their own narratives to explain what lies behind the quartos and Folio. They have said that Heminge and Condell meant to criticize only a few of the early quartos, the ones that offer much shorter and sometimes quite different, often garbled, versions of plays. Among the examples of these are the 1600 quarto of *Henry V* (the Folio offers a much fuller version) or the 1603 *Hamlet* quarto (in 1604 a different, much longer form of the play got into print as a quarto). Early in this century editors speculated that these questionable texts were produced when someone in the audience took notes from the plays' dialogue during performances and then employed "hack poets" to fill out the notes. The poor results were then sold to a publisher and presented in print as Shakespeare's plays. More recently this story has given way to another in which the shorter versions are said to be recreations from memory of Shakespeare's plays by actors who wanted to stage them in the provinces but lacked manuscript copies. Most of the quartos offer much better texts than these so-called bad quartos. Indeed, in most of the quartos we find texts that are at least equal to or better than what is printed in the Folio. Many of this century's Shakespeare enthusiasts have persuaded themselves that most of the quartos were set into type directly from Shakespeare's own papers, although there is nothing on which to base this conclusion except the desire for it to be true. Thus speculation continues about how the Shakespeare plays got to be printed. All that we have are the printed texts.

The book collector who was most successful in bringing together copies of the quartos and the First Folio was Henry Clay Folger, founder of the Folger Shakespeare Library in Washington, D.C. While it is estimated that there survive around the world only about 230 copies of the First Folio, Mr. Folger was able to acquire more than seventy-five copies, as well as a large number of fragments, for the library that bears his name. He also amassed a substantial number of quartos. For example, only fourteen copies of the First Quarto of *Love's Labor's Lost* are known to exist, and three are at the Folger Shakespeare Library. As a consequence of Mr. Folger's labors, twentieth-century scholars visiting the Folger Library have been able to learn a great deal about sixteenth- and seventeenth-century printing and, particularly, about the printing of Shakespeare's plays. And Mr. Folger did not stop at the First Folio, but collected many copies of later editions of Shakespeare, beginning with the Second Folio (1632), the Third (1663–64), and the Fourth (1685). Each of these later folios was based on its immediate predecessor and was edited anonymously. The first editor of Shakespeare whose name we know was Nicholas Rowe, whose first edition came out in 1709. Mr. Folger collected this edition and many, many more by Rowe's successors.

An Introduction to This Text

Much Ado About Nothing was first printed in 1600 as a quarto. This quarto is remarkable among early printed texts of Shakespeare's plays for the contrast it presents between the superb correctness of its dialogue and the many obvious errors and ambiguities in its stage directions and speech prefixes. Editors have found very little to require correction in the dialogue but are hard pressed to impose order on the stage directions and speech prefixes.

In 1623 the play was printed again, this time as part of the collection of Shakespeare's plays now known as the First Folio. The First Folio text is generally thought to be based on a lightly annotated copy of the First Quarto of 1600. Scholars used to believe that this very copy of the quarto was employed by Shakespeare's company in their theaters to regulate performance of the play. Even today, some scholars argue that whoever annotated the copy of the 1600 quarto used by the printers of the First Folio *Ado* must have referred to a manuscript of the play that had been used in the theater. To support this opinion, these scholars point to the substitution of what may be an actor's name (*"Iacke Wilson"*) for the name of the character Balthasar in one Folio stage direction, as well as to the Folio correction of one of the several errors in the quarto's stage directions and the addition of some stage directions for music. (It should be noted that the Folio also adds to the errors in the quarto's stage directions.) On the basis of this evidence, these scholars assert that the Folio *Ado* thus must be (indirectly) based on *the* manuscript that was used in the theater, and that the quarto must have been printed from Shakespeare's own manuscript—his so-called "foul papers." There is no reason, however, to believe that there existed only these two play manuscripts, since many different kinds of manuscripts of (non-Shakespearean) plays are still extant from the period. And there are just as good grounds for asserting that the quarto (rather than, or as well as, the Folio) may be based on a theatrical manuscript; the quarto speech prefixes, after all, contain the names of two quite well-known actors from Shakespeare's company—the clowns Will Kemp and Richard Cowley (see the Textual Notes to 4.2). To sum up: as today's scholars reexamine earlier accounts of the origins of the printed texts, we discover that these narratives are based on questionable evidence, and we become skeptical about ever identifying how the play assumed the forms in which it came to be printed.

The present edition is based directly on the earliest quarto of 1600.* (In view of the uncertainty surrounding the origin of alterations made to the quarto text in the Folio, after surveying the Folio changes, we have chosen largely to ignore them in preparing this edition.) For the convenience of the reader, we have generally modernized the punctuation and the spelling of the quarto. Sometimes we go so far as to modernize certain old forms of words; for example, when *a* means "he," we change it to *he;* we change *mo* to *more,* and *ye* to *you.* But it is not our practice in editing any of the plays to modernize words that sound distinctly different from modern forms. For example, when the early printed texts read *sith* or *apricocks* or *porpentine,* we have not modernized to *since, apricots, porcupine.* When the forms *an, and,* or *and if* appear instead of the modern form *if,* we have reduced *and* to *an* but have not changed any of these forms to their modern equivalent, *if.*

Although in general we have reduced the punctuation of the First Quarto to modern standards, we have left untouched in many cases one feature of its punctuation that arises from its use of the comma for many of the purposes nowadays filled by the semicolon, colon, and period. Take, for example, the First Quarto's punctuation of these words of the Friar in the play's last scene:

> All this amazement can I qualify,
> When after that the holy rites are ended,
> I'll tell you largely of fair Hero's death.

---

*We have also consulted the computerized text of the First Quarto provided by the Text Archive of the Oxford University Computing Centre, to which we are grateful.

As punctuated, the speech may be read in two ways because the "when" clause in the second line may be attached either to the first line or to the third. Depending on the attachment the reader makes, the speech may say either "after the rites I can mitigate all this amazement" or "after the rites I'll tell you all about Hero's death." There are no grounds for preferring one of these meanings to the other, and so, in such cases, we have not altered the First Quarto's punctuation, but instead we have presented the reader with the First Quarto's ambiguity.

Whenever we change the wording of the First Quarto or add anything to its stage directions, we mark the change by enclosing it in superior half-brackets (⌐ ¬). We want our readers to be immediately aware when we have intervened. (Only when we correct an obvious typographical error in the First Quarto does the change not get marked.) Whenever we change either the First Quarto's wording or its punctuation so that meaning changes, we list the change in the textual notes at the back of the book, even if all we have done is fix an obvious error.

We correct or regularize a number of the proper names. For example, when the Prince, usually called "Don Pedro," is twice referred to as "Peter," we change "Peter" to "Pedro." Or when Hero's waiting gentlewoman Ursula appears twice as "Ursley" in the First Quarto, we substitute "Ursula" on these occasions.

This edition differs from many earlier ones in its efforts to aid the reader in imagining the play as a performance rather than as a series of fictional events. Thus stage directions are written with reference to the stage. For example, in 4.1, after the character Hero has been accused of gross immorality, in the fiction of the play she faints (line 114). Thus traditional editions read *"Hero swoons."* But in performance the actor playing

Hero does not, of course, swoon; she merely slips down onto the stage. Since the stage directions in this edition are written with a view to performance, here our edition reads *"Hero falls."* Whenever it is reasonably certain, in our view, that a speech is accompanied by a particular action, we provide a stage direction describing the action. (Occasional exceptions to this rule occur when the action is so obvious that to add a stage direction would insult the reader.) Stage directions for the entrance of characters in mid-scene are placed so that the directions immediately precede the characters' participation in the scene, even though these entrances may appear somewhat earlier in the early printed texts. Whenever we move a stage direction, we record this change in the textual notes. Latin stage directions (e.g., *Exeunt*) are translated into English (e.g., *They exit*).

We expand the often severely abbreviated forms of names used as speech prefixes in early printed texts into the full names of the characters. We also regularize the speakers' names in speech prefixes, using only a single designation for each character, even though the early printed texts sometimes use a variety of designations. This task is a particularly challenging one for *Much Ado* because of the high incidence of inconsistency in the use of speech prefixes. The problem is particularly vexing, for example, in 3.3, where the Watchmen first appear. The quarto sometimes makes distinctions among these figures, using the speech prefixes *"Watch 1"* and *"Watch 2"*; but often it employs the thoroughly ambiguous speech prefix *"Watch."* Some recent editors have despaired of reducing these speech prefixes to any order and have simply used "A WATCHMAN" as the speech prefix throughout. While we sympathize with this practice, we have tried to help the reader by searching out patterns in the speeches that might be used to distinguish among the different Watchmen. We distinguish among three Watchmen. For one we use as his speech prefix the proper name given him in dialogue —Seacoal. He is chosen leader of the Watch, and we assign him speeches appropriate to a leader, mainly orders. To a second, whom we identify as "FIRST WATCHMAN" in speech prefixes, we give the speeches in which the word "deformed" is mistaken for the name of a criminal. The third we call "SECOND WATCHMAN." While the distinctions we observe among these three characters are not entirely consistent, we hope the attempt to sort out the quarto's ambiguity may be of some use to readers. Variations in the speech prefixes of the early printed text are recorded in the textual notes.

In the present edition, as well, we mark with a dash any change of address within a speech, unless a stage direction intervenes. When the *-ed* ending of a word is to be pronounced, we mark it with an accent. Like editors for the last two centuries, we print metrically linked lines in the following way:

BENEDICK
  Do not you love me?
BEATRICE   Why no, no more than reason.

However, when there are a number of short verse lines that can be linked in more than one way, we do not, with rare exceptions, indent any of them.

The Explanatory Notes

The notes that appear on the pages facing the text are designed to provide readers with the help they may need to enjoy the play. Whenever the meaning of a word in the text is not readily accessible in a good contemporary dictionary, we offer the meaning in a note. Sometimes we provide a note even when the relevant meaning is to be found in the dictionary but when the word has acquired since Shakespeare's time other potentially confusing meanings. In our notes, we try to offer modern synonyms for Shakespeare's words. We also try to indicate to the reader the connection between the word in the play and the modern synonym. For example, Shakespeare sometimes uses the word *head* to mean "source," but, for modern readers, there may be no connection evident between these two words. We provide the connection by explaining Shakespeare's usage as follows: "**head:** fountainhead, source." On some occasions, a whole phrase or clause needs explanation. Then we rephrase in our own words the difficult passage, and add at the end synonyms for individual words in the passage. When scholars have been unable to determine the meaning of a word or phrase, we acknowledge the uncertainty.

MUCH ADO
ABOUT NOTHING

MUCH ADO
ABOUT NOTHING

Characters in the Play

LEONATO, Governor of Messina
HERO, his daughter
BEATRICE, his niece
LEONATO'S BROTHER
MARGARET ⎱ *waiting gentlewomen to Hero*
URSULA ⎰

DON PEDRO, Prince of Aragon
COUNT CLAUDIO, a young lord from Florence
SIGNIOR BENEDICK, a gentleman from Padua
BALTHASAR
SIGNIOR ANTONIO

DON JOHN, Don Pedro's brother
BORACHIO ⎱ *Don John's followers*
CONRADE ⎰

DOGBERRY, Master Constable in Messina
VERGES, Dogberry's partner
GEORGE SEACOAL, leader of the Watch
FIRST WATCHMAN
SECOND WATCHMAN
SEXTON
FRIAR FRANCIS

MESSENGER to Leonato
MESSENGER to Don Pedro
BOY

Musicians, Lords, Attendants, Son to Leonato's brother

MUCH ADO
ABOUT NOTHING

ACT 1

1.1 The army of Don Pedro of Aragon arrives in Messina and is welcomed by Leonato, Messina's governor. Benedick of Padua, a soldier in Don Pedro's army, proclaims his enmity to love and engages in a skirmish of wits with Leonato's niece, Beatrice. Count Claudio, the hero of Don Pedro's just-ended war, falls in love with Leonato's daughter Hero and confesses his love to Don Pedro, who decides to woo Hero for Claudio.

---

0 SD. **Enter Leonato:** Early editions of the play include an entrance for a character named "Innogen," Leonato's "wife," who plays no part in the dialogue or action. See longer note, page 199.

2. **Aragon:** a region in northeast Spain; **Messina:** a port city in Sicily (See pages xiv–xv and xviii–xix.)

3. **this:** i.e., this time

6. **action:** battle

7. **sort:** rank; or, kind; **name:** fame, reputation

13. **remembered:** rewarded

14–15. **in . . . lamb:** i.e., while seeming young and weak   **figure:** appearance

15–16. **better bettered:** i.e., more greatly exceeded

18. **will:** i.e., who will

23. **badge:** sign; **bitterness:** i.e., suffering, anguish of heart

⌜ACT 1⌝

⌜Scene 1⌝

*Enter Leonato, Governor of Messina, Hero his daughter,
and Beatrice his niece, with a Messenger.*

LEONATO, ⌜*with a letter*⌝ I learn in this letter that Don
Pedro of Aragon comes this night to Messina.

MESSENGER He is very near by this. He was not three
leagues off when I left him.

LEONATO How many gentlemen have you lost in this   5
action?

MESSENGER But few of any sort, and none of name.

LEONATO A victory is twice itself when the achiever
brings home full numbers. I find here that Don
Pedro hath bestowed much honor on a young   10
Florentine called Claudio.

MESSENGER Much deserved on his part, and equally
remembered by Don Pedro. He hath borne himself
beyond the promise of his age, doing in the figure
of a lamb the feats of a lion. He hath indeed better   15
bettered expectation than you must expect of me to
tell you how.

LEONATO He hath an uncle here in Messina will be
very much glad of it.

MESSENGER I have already delivered him letters, and   20
there appears much joy in him, even so much that
joy could not show itself modest enough without a
badge of bitterness.

7

26. **kind:** (1) natural; (2) warmhearted; **kindness:** (1) kinship; (2) affection

27. **truer:** more honorable; more sincere

30. **Mountanto:** a fencing term (A *montant* is an upright blow or thrust.)

36. **pleasant:** merry

38. **bills:** handbills, posters

39. **Cupid:** the god of love, whose arrows cause people to fall in love (See pages 16 and 76.); **at the flight:** i.e., to an archery contest (perhaps to show that he could make women fall in love better than Cupid can); **Fool:** a servant who makes his living by amusing his aristocratic patron

40. **subscribed for Cupid:** i.e., signed on Cupid's behalf

41. **bird-bolt:** a blunt-headed arrow used to shoot birds

42. **he:** i.e., Benedick

45. **tax:** i.e., take to task, criticize

46. **meet:** even

49. **hath holp:** i.e., has helped

50. **trencherman:** eater (also, insultingly, "parasitical dependent")

51. **stomach:** Beatrice plays on **stomach** as meaning both "appetite" and "courage."

57–58. **stuffed man:** perhaps, a figure stuffed with cotton to resemble a human

LEONATO Did he break out into tears?

MESSENGER In great measure.   25

LEONATO A kind overflow of kindness. There are no
faces truer than those that are so washed. How
much better is it to weep at joy than to joy at
weeping!

BEATRICE I pray you, is Signior Mountanto returned   30
from the wars or no?

MESSENGER I know none of that name, lady. There
was none such in the army of any sort.

LEONATO What is he that you ask for, niece?

HERO My cousin means Signior Benedick of Padua.   35

MESSENGER O, he's returned, and as pleasant as ever
he was.

BEATRICE He set up his bills here in Messina and
challenged Cupid at the flight, and my uncle's Fool,
reading the challenge, subscribed for Cupid and   40
challenged him at the bird-bolt. I pray you, how
many hath he killed and eaten in these wars? But
how many hath he killed? For indeed I promised to
eat all of his killing.

LEONATO Faith, niece, you tax Signior Benedick too   45
much, but he'll be meet with you, I doubt it not.

MESSENGER He hath done good service, lady, in these
wars.

BEATRICE You had musty victual, and he hath holp to
eat it. He is a very valiant trencherman; he hath an   50
excellent stomach.

MESSENGER And a good soldier too, lady.

BEATRICE And a good soldier to a lady, but what is he
to a lord?

MESSENGER A lord to a lord, a man to a man, stuffed   55
with all honorable virtues.

BEATRICE It is so indeed. He is no less than a stuffed
man, but for the stuffing—well, we are all mortal.

61. **skirmish of wit:** i.e., exchange of verbal thrusts

64. **five wits:** i.e., the mental faculties of human beings; **halting:** limping

65. **with:** i.e., by

67. **a difference:** i.e., a mark on a coat of arms that indicates one's rank within a family

70–71. **sworn brother:** i.e., brother-in-arms, friend sworn to support one as if one's brother

75. **block:** fashion (literally: a mold for shaping a felt hat)

76–77. **in your books:** i.e., in your favor

78. **An:** if; **study:** i.e., library

80. **squarer:** fighter, quarreler

84. **he:** i.e., Benedick

86. **taker:** i.e., victim; **presently:** immediately

89. **hold:** i.e., remain

93. **is approached:** i.e., has come near, has arrived

Coat of arms showing a mark of "difference." (1.1.67)
From Ralph Brooke, *A catalogue . . . of the kings . . .* (1622).

LEONATO You must not, sir, mistake my niece. There is
a kind of merry war betwixt Signior Benedick and   60
her. They never meet but there's a skirmish of wit
between them.

BEATRICE Alas, he gets nothing by that. In our last
conflict, four of his five wits went halting off, and
now is the whole man governed with one, so that if   65
he have wit enough to keep himself warm, let him
bear it for a difference between himself and his
horse, for it is all the wealth that he hath left to
be known a reasonable creature. Who is his companion now? He hath every month a new sworn   70
brother.

MESSENGER Is 't possible?

BEATRICE Very easily possible. He wears his faith but
as the fashion of his hat; it ever changes with the
next block.   75

MESSENGER I see, lady, the gentleman is not in your
books.

BEATRICE No. An he were, I would burn my study. But
I pray you, who is his companion? Is there no
young squarer now that will make a voyage with   80
him to the devil?

MESSENGER He is most in the company of the right
noble Claudio.

BEATRICE O Lord, he will hang upon him like a
disease! He is sooner caught than the pestilence,   85
and the taker runs presently mad. God help the
noble Claudio! If he have caught the Benedick, it
will cost him a thousand pound ere he be cured.

MESSENGER I will hold friends with you, lady.

BEATRICE Do, good friend.   90

LEONATO You will never run mad, niece.

BEATRICE No, not till a hot January.

MESSENGER Don Pedro is approached.

96. **cost:** expense (here, the expense of the army's visit, which Leonato, as the Prince's host, must bear); **encounter:** come to meet

101. **charge:** (1) duty; (2) expense

107. **have it full:** perhaps, are well answered   **full:** completely

109. **fathers herself:** i.e., proclaims in her looks who her father is

119. **meet:** suitable, appropriate

120. **convert to:** turn into

124. **would:** wish

At "the flight." (1.1.39)
From Gilles Corrozet, *Hecatongraphie* . . . (1543).

Enter Don Pedro, ⌜Prince of Aragon, with⌝ Claudio,
Benedick, Balthasar, and John the Bastard.

PRINCE   Good Signior Leonato, are you come to meet
your trouble? The fashion of the world is to avoid   95
cost, and you encounter it.

LEONATO   Never came trouble to my house in the
likeness of your Grace, for trouble being gone,
comfort should remain, but when you depart from
me, sorrow abides and happiness takes his leave.   100

PRINCE   You embrace your charge too willingly. ⌜*Turn-*
ing to Hero.⌝ I think this is your daughter.

LEONATO   Her mother hath many times told me so.

BENEDICK   Were you in doubt, sir, that you asked her?

LEONATO   Signior Benedick, no, for then were you a   105
child.

PRINCE   You have it full, Benedick. We may guess by
this what you are, being a man. Truly the lady
fathers herself.—Be happy, lady, for you are like
an honorable father.   110
⌜*Leonato and the Prince move aside.*⌝

BENEDICK   If Signior Leonato be her father, she would
not have his head on her shoulders for all Messina,
as like him as she is.

BEATRICE   I wonder that you will still be talking, Signior Benedick, nobody marks you.   115

BENEDICK   What, my dear Lady Disdain! Are you yet
living?

BEATRICE   Is it possible disdain should die while she
hath such meet food to feed it as Signior Benedick?
Courtesy itself must convert to disdain if you come   120
in her presence.

BENEDICK   Then is courtesy a turncoat. But it is certain I am loved of all ladies, only you excepted; and
I would I could find in my heart that I had not a
hard heart, for truly I love none.   125

127. **else:** otherwise

128. **cold blood:** i.e., blood not warmed by passion

128–29. **I am . . . that:** i.e., in that (i.e., loving no one) you and I agree

131. **still:** always

132–33. **predestinate:** i.e., predestined, fated

134–35. **an 'twere:** if it were

135. **were:** i.e., is

136. **you . . . parrot-teacher:** i.e., you jabber (or, repeat yourself) expertly, as if teaching a parrot to talk

137. **of my tongue:** perhaps, who speaks like me; or, perhaps, who is able to speak

137–38. **a beast of yours:** perhaps, who speaks like you; or, perhaps, who cannot speak (i.e., is a dumb beast); or, perhaps, who speaks hypocritically (i.e., with a "forked tongue")

140. **so good a continuer:** i.e., was so tireless in running

142. **a jade's trick:** i.e., an unfair or foolish conclusion (An untrustworthy horse [a **jade**] might trick its rider by pulling its neck out of the halter or by stopping suddenly, as Benedick has just done.)

143. **of old:** i.e., from the past

150–51. **shall . . . forsworn:** i.e., will not have sworn falsely, perjured yourself

156. **Please it . . . lead:** i.e., will you please lead

158. **note:** notice, pay attention to

BEATRICE A dear happiness to women. They would
else have been troubled with a pernicious suitor. I
thank God and my cold blood I am of your humor
for that. I had rather hear my dog bark at a crow
than a man swear he loves me.   130
BENEDICK God keep your Ladyship still in that mind,
so some gentleman or other shall 'scape a predestinate scratched face.
BEATRICE Scratching could not make it worse an
'twere such a face as yours were.   135
BENEDICK Well, you are a rare parrot-teacher.
BEATRICE A bird of my tongue is better than a beast of
yours.
BENEDICK I would my horse had the speed of your
tongue and so good a continuer, but keep your   140
way, i' God's name, I have done.
BEATRICE You always end with a jade's trick. I know
you of old.
                ⌜*Leonato and the Prince come forward.*⌝
PRINCE That is the sum of all, Leonato.—Signior
Claudio and Signior Benedick, my dear friend   145
Leonato hath invited you all. I tell him we shall stay
here at the least a month, and he heartily prays
some occasion may detain us longer. I dare swear
he is no hypocrite, but prays from his heart.
LEONATO If you swear, my lord, you shall not be   150
forsworn. ⌜*To Don John.*⌝ Let me bid you welcome,
my lord, being reconciled to the Prince your broth-
er, I owe you all duty.
DON JOHN I thank you. I am not of many words, but I
thank you.   155
LEONATO Please it your Grace lead on?
PRINCE Your hand, Leonato. We will go together.
                ⌜*All*⌝ *exit except Benedick and Claudio.*
CLAUDIO Benedick, didst thou note the daughter of
Signior Leonato?

161. **modest:** well-mannered

167. **methinks:** it seems to me; **low:** i.e., short

173. **in sport:** joking

179. **sad:** serious

179–80. **flouting jack:** mocking fellow

180. **Cupid . . . hare-finder:** Since Cupid is blind, he would not be a good finder of hares.

181. **Vulcan . . . carpenter:** Vulcan is blacksmith of the gods, not a carpenter.

182. **go . . . song:** i.e., join with you in singing the tune

187. **possessed with a fury:** i.e., as if under the control of one of the Furies, dread goddesses sent from hell to avenge crimes

194–95. **but . . . suspicion:** i.e., who will refuse to marry because of the fear that his wife will prove unfaithful and make him a cuckold (A cuckold is imaged as growing horns, which his cap may hide. See page 32 and longer note, page 199.)

"Cupid is a good hare-finder." (1.1.180)
From Francesco Petrarca, *Opera* . . . (1508).

BENEDICK   I noted her not, but I looked on her.   160
CLAUDIO   Is she not a modest young lady?
BENEDICK   Do you question me as an honest man
     should do, for my simple true judgment? Or would
     you have me speak after my custom, as being a
     professed tyrant to their sex?   165
CLAUDIO   No, I pray thee, speak in sober judgment.
BENEDICK   Why, i' faith, methinks she's too low for a
     high praise, too brown for a fair praise, and too
     little for a great praise. Only this commendation I
     can afford her, that were she other than she is, she   170
     were unhandsome, and being no other but as she is,
     I do not like her.
CLAUDIO   Thou thinkest I am in sport. I pray thee tell
     me truly how thou lik'st her.
BENEDICK   Would you buy her that you enquire after   175
     her?
CLAUDIO   Can the world buy such a jewel?
BENEDICK   Yea, and a case to put it into. But speak you
     this with a sad brow? Or do you play the flouting
     jack, to tell us Cupid is a good hare-finder and   180
     Vulcan a rare carpenter? Come, in what key shall a
     man take you to go in the song?
CLAUDIO   In mine eye she is the sweetest lady that ever
     I looked on.
BENEDICK   I can see yet without spectacles, and I see   185
     no such matter. There's her cousin, an she were not
     possessed with a fury, exceeds her as much in
     beauty as the first of May doth the last of December.
     But I hope you have no intent to turn husband, have
     you?   190
CLAUDIO   I would scarce trust myself, though I had
     sworn the contrary, if Hero would be my wife.
BENEDICK   Is 't come to this? In faith, hath not the
     world one man but he will wear his cap with
     suspicion? Shall I never see a bachelor of three-   195

196. Go to: an expression of impatience

196–98. wilt needs . . . Sundays: Benedick attacks marriage with the image of the **yoke** of marriage, the yoke's **print** (i.e., imprint, impression), and its depressing impact on one's leisure time (**sigh away Sundays**). See page 174.

206. dumb: mute, speechless

211. If . . . uttered: i.e., if this were true, it would be told to you this way

212. old tale: Benedick refers to a fairy tale about a "Mr. Fox," in which the refrain Benedick quotes plays a key role.

215. passion: feeling, desire

219. fetch me in: trick me

227–50. opinion . . . faith: Benedick's references to **fire** and **the stake** introduce the idea of religious heresy and its punishments, picked up with such words as **obstinate heretic** and **fall from this faith.**

Matrimonium:

The marriage yoke. (1.1.197)
From Henry Peacham, *Minerua Britanna* . . . (1612).

score again? Go to, i' faith, an thou wilt needs thrust
thy neck into a yoke, wear the print of it, and sigh
away Sundays. Look, Don Pedro is returned to seek
you.

Enter Don Pedro, ⌐Prince of Aragon.⌐

PRINCE   What secret hath held you here that you fol-   200
lowed not to Leonato's?
BENEDICK   I would your Grace would constrain me to
tell.
PRINCE   I charge thee on thy allegiance.
BENEDICK   You hear, Count Claudio, I can be secret as   205
a dumb man, I would have you think so, but on my
allegiance—mark you this, on my allegiance—he
is in love. With who? Now, that is your Grace's part.
Mark how short his answer is: with Hero, Leonato's
short daughter.   210
CLAUDIO   If this were so, so were it uttered.
BENEDICK   Like the old tale, my lord: "It is not so, nor
'twas not so, but, indeed, God forbid it should be
so."
CLAUDIO   If my passion change not shortly, God forbid   215
it should be otherwise.
PRINCE   Amen, if you love her, for the lady is very well
worthy.
CLAUDIO   You speak this to fetch me in, my lord.
PRINCE   By my troth, I speak my thought.   220
CLAUDIO   And in faith, my lord, I spoke mine.
BENEDICK   And by my two faiths and troths, my lord, I
spoke mine.
CLAUDIO   That I love her, I feel.
PRINCE   That she is worthy, I know.   225
BENEDICK   That I neither feel how she should be loved
nor know how she should be worthy is the opinion
that fire cannot melt out of me. I will die in it at the
stake.

230–31. **in the despite of:** i.e., in disdaining

232. **but in:** i.e., except through

236–38. **have a recheat . . . baldrick:** i.e., wear the horns of a cuckold **recheat:** notes of a hunting horn **winded:** sounded, blown (See page 46.) **baldrick:** belt for holding bugles, swords, etc. Here the baldrick is **invisible** because the bugle is the purely imaginary horn of the cuckold. (See longer note to 1.1.194–95, page 199, and picture on page 32.)

241. **fine:** conclusion; **the finer:** i.e., better dressed

245–46. **lose . . . drinking:** In Elizabethan thinking, sighs draw blood from the heart while wine restores it.

248–49. **for . . . Cupid:** i.e., in place of a signboard with a picture of blind Cupid

251. **argument:** theme of discussion

252. **do:** i.e., **fall from this faith; hang . . . cat:** A cat hung in a wicker or leather basket was sometimes used as a target.

254. **Adam:** The archer Adam Bell was the hero of an old ballad.

255. **try:** test (Proverb: "Time tries [i.e., tests] all things.")

256. **In . . . yoke:** proverbial (See page 68.)

259. **let . . . painted:** i.e., have a picture made of me (with my horns)

261. **sign:** i.e., picture (on the signboard)

264. **horn-mad:** i.e., raving mad (with a pun on his cuckold's horns)

PRINCE Thou wast ever an obstinate heretic in the 230
despite of beauty.

CLAUDIO And never could maintain his part but in the
force of his will.

BENEDICK That a woman conceived me, I thank her;
that she brought me up, I likewise give her most 235
humble thanks. But that I will have a recheat
winded in my forehead or hang my bugle in an
invisible baldrick, all women shall pardon me.
Because I will not do them the wrong to mistrust
any, I will do myself the right to trust none. And the 240
fine is, for the which I may go the finer, I will live a
bachelor.

PRINCE I shall see thee, ere I die, look pale with love.

BENEDICK With anger, with sickness, or with hunger,
my lord, not with love. Prove that ever I lose more 245
blood with love than I will get again with drinking,
pick out mine eyes with a ballad-maker's pen and
hang me up at the door of a brothel house for the
sign of blind Cupid.

PRINCE Well, if ever thou dost fall from this faith, thou 250
wilt prove a notable argument.

BENEDICK If I do, hang me in a bottle like a cat and
shoot at me, and he that hits me, let him be clapped
on the shoulder and called Adam.

PRINCE Well, as time shall try. 255
In time the savage bull doth bear the yoke.

BENEDICK The savage bull may, but if ever the sensible
Benedick bear it, pluck off the bull's horns and set
them in my forehead, and let me be vilely painted,
and in such great letters as they write "Here is good 260
horse to hire" let them signify under my sign "Here
you may see Benedick the married man."

CLAUDIO If this should ever happen, thou wouldst be
horn-mad.

265. **spent . . . quiver:** used up his quiverful of arrows

266. **Venice:** a city famous at the time for its courtesans

268. **temporize:** adapt yourself, change

269. **repair:** go

270. **Commend me:** offer my respects

271. **fail him:** i.e., fail (to appear)

273. **matter:** i.e., subject matter, material

274. **embassage:** embassy, mission; **commit you:** a polite phrase at parting, which the Prince and Claudio treat as if it were the complimentary close of a letter

275. **tuition:** protection

280. **guarded:** trimmed

281. **guards:** ornaments, trimmings; **but . . . neither:** i.e., only loosely sewn on or connected

282. **flout old ends:** banter with bits and pieces of conventional language

286. **apt:** inclined; ready

290. **affect:** like

292. **onward:** forward; **action:** military engagement

296. **now:** i.e., now that

PRINCE   Nay, if Cupid have not spent all his quiver in   265
Venice, thou wilt quake for this shortly.

BENEDICK   I look for an earthquake too, then.

PRINCE   Well, you will temporize with the hours. In the
meantime, good Signior Benedick, repair to Leonato's. Commend me to him, and tell him I will not   270
fail him at supper, for indeed he hath made great
preparation.

BENEDICK   I have almost matter enough in me for such
an embassage, and so I commit you—

CLAUDIO   To the tuition of God. From my house, if I had   275
it—

PRINCE   The sixth of July. Your loving friend, Benedick.

BENEDICK   Nay, mock not, mock not. The body of your
discourse is sometimes guarded with fragments,   280
and the guards are but slightly basted on neither.
Ere you flout old ends any further, examine your
conscience. And so I leave you.   *He exits.*

CLAUDIO
My liege, your Highness now may do me good.

PRINCE
My love is thine to teach. Teach it but how,   285
And thou shalt see how apt it is to learn
Any hard lesson that may do thee good.

CLAUDIO
Hath Leonato any son, my lord?

PRINCE
No child but Hero; she's his only heir.
Dost thou affect her, Claudio?   290

CLAUDIO   O, my lord,
When you went onward on this ended action,
I looked upon her with a soldier's eye,
That liked, but had a rougher task in hand
Than to drive liking to the name of love.   295
But now I am returned and that war thoughts

301. **presently:** soon

304. **break with:** reveal (the matter) to

306. **twist:** i.e., spin (literally, to form a thread by combining fibers)

308. **his complexion:** its outward signs

310. **salved:** i.e., explained; or, smoothed it over; **treatise:** story

311. **What . . . bridge:** i.e., why should the bridge be; **flood:** river

312. **fairest grant:** best gift: **the necessity:** i.e., that which is needed

313. **Look what:** whatever

315. **reveling:** i.e., masked dancing

318. **in her bosom:** i.e., privately; **unclasp:** i.e., open (as if the heart were a book fastened, as books often were at the time, with metal clasps)

321. **after:** i.e., afterward; **break:** i.e., speak, reveal (my mind)

323. **presently:** immediately

A book with clasps. (1.1.318)
From *Notitia vtraque cum Orientis* . . . (1552).

Have left their places vacant, in their rooms
Come thronging soft and delicate desires,
All prompting me how fair young Hero is,
Saying I liked her ere I went to wars.   300

PRINCE
Thou wilt be like a lover presently
And tire the hearer with a book of words.
If thou dost love fair Hero, cherish it,
And I will break with her and with her father,
And thou shalt have her. Was 't not to this end   305
That thou began'st to twist so fine a story?

CLAUDIO
How sweetly you do minister to love,
That know love's grief by his complexion!
But lest my liking might too sudden seem,
I would have salved it with a longer treatise.   310

PRINCE
What need the bridge much broader than the flood?
The fairest grant is the necessity.
Look what will serve is fit. 'Tis once, thou lovest,
And I will fit thee with the remedy.
I know we shall have reveling tonight.   315
I will assume thy part in some disguise
And tell fair Hero I am Claudio,
And in her bosom I'll unclasp my heart
And take her hearing prisoner with the force
And strong encounter of my amorous tale.   320
Then after to her father will I break,
And the conclusion is, she shall be thine.
In practice let us put it presently.

                                        They exit.

1.2 Leonato is given a garbled account of the conversation between Don Pedro and Claudio, and is led to believe that Don Pedro wishes to marry Hero.

———————

0 SD. brother to Leonato: Most editors assume that the **old man** is the same character as the Signior Antonio who appears with the maskers in 2.1. Our reasons for questioning this assumption are explained in the longer note on pages 199–200.

1. cousin: i.e., kinsman, nephew (This character is mentioned only in this scene.)

6. they: i.e., the **news** (originally a plural noun)

7. stamps them: i.e., shows or proves them to be (literally, impresses or prints them)

8. cover: outer binding (as on a book)

9–10. a thick-pleached alley: a walkway bordered with intertwined boughs (See page 223.)

10. orchard: formal garden (See page 74.)

11. man: servant; **discovered:** revealed

14–15. take . . . top: a proverb meaning "seize the moment" (**Present time,** or Occasion, was often pictured as having a single lock of hair growing from the top of his or her head.)

15–16. break . . . it: reveal (the matter) to you

17. wit: intelligence

22. withal: i.e., with it

23. peradventure: perhaps

25–26. I cry you mercy: a polite phrase of apology

⌜Scene 2⌝
*Enter Leonato, ⌜meeting⌝ an old man, brother to
Leonato.*

LEONATO   How now, brother, where is my cousin, your
son? Hath he provided this music?

LEONATO'S BROTHER   He is very busy about it. But,
brother, I can tell you strange news that you yet
dreamt not of.   5

LEONATO   Are they good?

LEONATO'S BROTHER   As the events stamps them, but
they have a good cover; they show well outward.
The Prince and Count Claudio, walking in a thick-
pleached alley in mine orchard, were thus much   10
overheard by a man of mine: the Prince discovered
to Claudio that he loved my niece your daughter and
meant to acknowledge it this night in a dance, and if
he found her accordant, he meant to take the
present time by the top and instantly break with you   15
of it.

LEONATO   Hath the fellow any wit that told you this?

LEONATO'S BROTHER   A good sharp fellow. I will send
for him, and question him yourself.

LEONATO   No, no, we will hold it as a dream till it   20
appear itself. But I will acquaint my daughter
withal, that she may be the better prepared for an
answer, if peradventure this be true. Go you and tell
her of it.

⌜*Enter Antonio's son, with a Musician and Attendants.*⌝

Cousins, you know what you have to do.—O, I cry   25
you mercy, friend. Go you with me and I will use
your skill.—Good cousin, have a care this busy
time.

They exit.

1.3 Don John, Don Pedro's brother, receives a true account of Don Pedro's plan to woo Hero for Claudio. Resentful of both Don Pedro and Claudio, who have defeated him in the just-ended war, Don John hopes to find a way to block the marriage.

---

1. **What the goodyear:** an exclamation of no known meaning
2. **out of measure:** beyond all limits, excessively
3. **measure:** limit
4. **breeds:** causes (it)
9. **sufferance:** endurance
11. **born under Saturn:** i.e., born when the planet Saturn was in the ascendant, and thus "saturnine" or gloomy
11–12. **apply . . . mischief:** i.e., use sayings from moral philosophy to cure a deadly disease
14. **stomach:** appetite, hunger
16. **tend on:** take care of, serve
17. **claw . . . humor:** flatter or fawn upon any man **humor:** mood, whim
19. **controlment:** restraint
20. **of late:** lately; **stood out against:** opposed
21. **grace:** favor
24. **frame:** fashion
25. **canker:** prickly wild rose (*Rosa canina*)
26. **blood: Blood** was considered the seat of emotions and passions.
27. **of:** i.e., by; **fashion a carriage:** i.e., assume a manner
31. **enfranchised:** freed; **with a clog:** i.e., weighted down as if by a heavy block (See page 158.)
32. **decreed:** resolved

⌜Scene 3⌝
Enter Sir John the Bastard, and Conrade, his
companion.

CONRADE What the goodyear, my lord, why are you
thus out of measure sad?
DON JOHN There is no measure in the occasion that
breeds. Therefore the sadness is without limit.
CONRADE You should hear reason.   5
DON JOHN And when I have heard it, what blessing
brings it?
CONRADE If not a present remedy, at least a patient
sufferance.
DON JOHN I wonder that thou, being, as thou sayst thou   10
art, born under Saturn, goest about to apply a moral
medicine to a mortifying mischief. I cannot hide
what I am. I must be sad when I have cause, and
smile at no man's jests; eat when I have stomach,
and wait for no man's leisure; sleep when I am   15
drowsy, and tend on no man's business; laugh when
I am merry, and claw no man in his humor.
CONRADE Yea, but you must not make the full show of
this till you may do it without controlment. You
have of late stood out against your brother, and he   20
hath ta'en you newly into his grace, where it is
impossible you should take true root but by the fair
weather that you make yourself. It is needful that
you frame the season for your own harvest.
DON JOHN I had rather be a canker in a hedge than a   25
rose in his grace, and it better fits my blood to be
disdained of all than to fashion a carriage to rob
love from any. In this, though I cannot be said to be
a flattering honest man, it must not be denied but I
am a plain-dealing villain. I am trusted with a   30
muzzle and enfranchised with a clog; therefore I
have decreed not to sing in my cage. If I had my

37. **I make . . . only:** i.e., I make every use of it, for it is all that I use

42. **intelligence:** information

45. **What . . . fool:** i.e., what kind of fool is he

47. **Marry:** i.e., indeed (originally an oath "by the Virgin Mary")

50. **proper squire:** here, a term of contempt **proper:** fine, handsome

54. **forward:** precocious; **March chick:** i.e., young one

56. **entertained for:** employed as; **perfumer:** i.e., fumigator

57. **smoking:** i.e., using smoke to fumigate; **comes me:** i.e., come

58. **sad conference:** serious conversation

59. **whipped me:** i.e., whipped; **arras:** a hanging screen of rich tapestry fabric

64. **start-up:** upstart, parvenu

65. **cross:** impede, thwart (An additional meaning, "to make the sign of the cross," is suggested with the words **bless myself** in the next line.)

A censer "smoking a musty room." (1.3.57)
From Giovanni Ferro, *Teatro d'imprese* . . . (1623).

mouth, I would bite; if I had my liberty, I would do
my liking. In the meantime, let me be that I am, and
seek not to alter me.   35

CONRADE   Can you make no use of your discontent?

DON JOHN   I make all use of it, for I use it only. Who
comes here?

Enter Borachio.

What news, Borachio?

BORACHIO   I came yonder from a great supper. The   40
Prince your brother is royally entertained by
Leonato, and I can give you intelligence of an
intended marriage.

DON JOHN   Will it serve for any model to build mischief
on? What is he for a fool that betroths himself to   45
unquietness?

BORACHIO   Marry, it is your brother's right hand.

DON JOHN   Who, the most exquisite Claudio?

BORACHIO   Even he.

DON JOHN   A proper squire. And who, and who? Which   50
way looks he?

BORACHIO   Marry, on Hero, the daughter and heir of
Leonato.

DON JOHN   A very forward March chick! How came you
to this?   55

BORACHIO   Being entertained for a perfumer, as I was
smoking a musty room, comes me the Prince and
Claudio, hand in hand, in sad conference. I
whipped me behind the arras, and there heard it
agreed upon that the Prince should woo Hero for   60
himself, and having obtained her, give her to Count
Claudio.

DON JOHN   Come, come, let us thither. This may prove
food to my displeasure. That young start-up hath
all the glory of my overthrow. If I can cross him any   65

66. **sure:** i.e., secure, loyal
71. **prove:** test, check out

A cuckold. (1.1.194–95)
From *Bagford Ballads* (printed 1868–99).

way, I bless myself every way. You are both sure, and
will assist me?

CONRADE   To the death, my lord.

DON JOHN   Let us to the great supper. Their cheer is the
greater that I am subdued. Would the cook were o'   70
my mind! Shall we go prove what's to be done?

BORACHIO   We'll wait upon your Lordship.

⌜*They*⌝ *exit.*

MUCH ADO
ABOUT NOTHING

ACT 2

2.1 Don Pedro and his soldiers, disguised in masks, dance with the ladies of Leonato's household. While Don Pedro woos Hero, Beatrice mocks Benedick. After the dance, Don John distresses Claudio by telling him that Don Pedro has won Hero's love. When Claudio learns that Hero has been won in his name, he wants to marry her immediately. Leonato insists that at least a week is needed to prepare for the wedding. Don Pedro proposes that the intervening time be used to trick Benedick and Beatrice into falling in love.

---

3. **tartly:** sour
6. **He . . . man:** i.e., an excellent man would be one
8. **image:** i.e., statue, picture
9. **my lady's eldest son:** i.e., a pampered boy
10. **tattling:** chattering, talking aimlessly
18. **By my troth:** a mild oath by one's faith
19. **shrewd:** malicious, harsh; **of thy tongue:** i.e., with what you say
20. **In faith:** a mild oath; **curst:** a word used to describe women considered quarrelsome, talkative, or sharp-tongued
22–23. **God . . . horns:** a proverb that supposedly illustrates God's providence (In the proverb, **curst** means ill-tempered, vicious.)

⌜ACT 2⌝

⌜Scene 1⌝

Enter Leonato, his brother, Hero his daughter, and
Beatrice his niece, ⌜with Ursula and Margaret.⌝

LEONATO Was not Count John here at supper?

LEONATO'S BROTHER   I saw him not.

BEATRICE How tartly that gentleman looks! I never
can see him but I am heartburned an hour after.

HERO He is of a very melancholy disposition.   5

BEATRICE He were an excellent man that were made
just in the midway between him and Benedick. The
one is too like an image and says nothing, and the
other too like my lady's eldest son, evermore
tattling.   10

LEONATO Then half Signior Benedick's tongue in
Count John's mouth, and half Count John's melancholy in Signior Benedick's face—

BEATRICE With a good leg and a good foot, uncle, and
money enough in his purse, such a man would win   15
any woman in the world if he could get her goodwill.

LEONATO By my troth, niece, thou wilt never get thee a
husband if thou be so shrewd of thy tongue.

LEONATO'S BROTHER   In faith, she's too curst.   20

BEATRICE Too curst is more than curst. I shall lessen
God's sending that way, for it is said "God sends a

37

27. **Just:** i.e., exactly; **send . . . husband:** The man whose wife is unfaithful supposedly grows horns. Beatrice jokes that the only horns God might send her would grow on her husband's forehead.

30–31. **lie in the woolen:** i.e., sleep with a wool blanket next to my skin

32. **light on:** come upon unexpectedly

35. **waiting gentlewoman:** a gentlewoman who serves a lady of higher rank

40. **earnest:** a small payment to seal a bargain; **of:** i.e., from; **bearherd:** keeper of a performing bear

40–41. **lead his apes into hell:** Proverbial: "Those who die maids do lead apes in hell," meaning that women who do not marry are punished in the afterlife. **his apes:** Bearherds often had performing apes as well as bears.

47–48. **Saint Peter . . . sit:** These puzzling lines have the general sense that Saint Peter, in Beatrice's fantasy, will direct her to the bachelors' part of heaven.

A bearherd. (2.1.40)
From Jacobus a. Bruck, *Emblemata moralia* . . . (1615).

curst cow short horns," but to a cow too curst, he
sends none.

LEONATO   So, by being too curst, God will send you no   25
horns.

BEATRICE   Just, if he send me no husband, for the
which blessing I am at him upon my knees every
morning and evening. Lord, I could not endure a
husband with a beard on his face. I had rather lie in   30
the woolen!

LEONATO   You may light on a husband that hath no
beard.

BEATRICE   What should I do with him? Dress him in my
apparel and make him my waiting gentlewoman?   35
He that hath a beard is more than a youth, and he
that hath no beard is less than a man; and he that is
more than a youth is not for me, and he that is less
than a man, I am not for him. Therefore I will even
take sixpence in earnest of the bearherd, and lead   40
his apes into hell.

LEONATO   Well then, go you into hell?

BEATRICE   No, but to the gate, and there will the devil
meet me like an old cuckold with horns on his
head, and say "Get you to heaven, Beatrice, get you   45
to heaven; here's no place for you maids." So deliver
I up my apes and away to Saint Peter; for the
heavens, he shows me where the bachelors sit, and
there live we as merry as the day is long.

LEONATO'S BROTHER, ⌜to Hero⌝   Well, niece, I trust you   50
will be ruled by your father.

BEATRICE   Yes, faith, it is my cousin's duty to make
curtsy and say "Father, as it please you." But yet for
all that, cousin, let him be a handsome fellow, or
else make another curtsy and say "Father, as it   55
please me."

LEONATO   Well, niece, I hope to see you one day fitted
with a husband.

59. **metal:** i.e., the "stuff" of which a person is made (with wordplay on *mettle* as referring to a person's character and on *metal* as referring to the physical body)

61. **dust:** See Genesis 2.7: "the Lord God formed man of the dust of the ground."

63. **I'll none:** i.e., I'll have no husband

64. **match in:** i.e., marry

66. **in that kind:** i.e., in that regard

69. **in good time:** (1) at the proper time; (2) with the proper rhythm

70. **important:** importunate; **measure:** moderation; rhythm

72. **repenting:** regretting; **jig:** lively dance

73. **measure:** grave or stately dance, such as a pavan; **cinquepace:** i.e., galliard, a popular lively dance (pronounced "sink-a-pace"); **first suit:** i.e., wooing

74. **fantastical:** quaint, grotesque

76. **state:** i.e., stateliness; **ancientry:** old-fashioned style; **repentance:** regret

79. **passing:** surpassingly, extremely

82–83. **Make good room:** i.e., step aside

83 SD. **Drum:** i.e., a person with a small drum or tabor (See longer note, page 200.); **Signior Antonio:** See longer note to 1.2.0 SD, page 199.

84. **walk a bout:** i.e., dance a round

BEATRICE Not till God make men of some other metal
than earth. Would it not grieve a woman to be   60
overmastered with a piece of valiant dust? To make
an account of her life to a clod of wayward marl?
No, uncle, I'll none. Adam's sons are my brethren,
and truly I hold it a sin to match in my kindred.
LEONATO, ⌐to Hero⌐ Daughter, remember what I told   65
you. If the Prince do solicit you in that kind, you
know your answer.
BEATRICE The fault will be in the music, cousin, if you
be not wooed in good time. If the Prince be too
important, tell him there is measure in everything,   70
and so dance out the answer. For hear me, Hero,
wooing, wedding, and repenting is as a Scotch jig, a
measure, and a cinquepace. The first suit is hot and
hasty like a Scotch jig, and full as fantastical; the
wedding, mannerly modest as a measure, full of   75
state and ancientry; and then comes repentance,
and with his bad legs falls into the cinquepace faster
and faster till he sink into his grave.
LEONATO Cousin, you apprehend passing shrewdly.
BEATRICE I have a good eye, uncle; I can see a church   80
by daylight.
LEONATO The revelers are entering, brother. Make
good room. ⌐Leonato and his brother step aside.⌐

Enter, ⌐with a Drum,⌐ Prince Pedro, Claudio, and
Benedick, ⌐Signior Antonio,⌐ and Balthasar, ⌐all in
masks, with Borachio and Don⌐ John.

PRINCE, ⌐to Hero⌐ Lady, will you walk a bout with your
friend?   ⌐They begin to dance.⌐   85
HERO So you walk softly, and look sweetly, and say
nothing, I am yours for the walk, and especially
when I walk away.
PRINCE With me in your company?
HERO I may say so when I please.   90

92. **favor:** face; **defend:** forbid
92-93. **the lute ... case:** i.e., your face should resemble your mask
94-95. **My ... Jove:** In classical mythology, Jove, king of the Roman gods, was entertained by a poor man, Philemon, in his thatched hut. **visor:** mask
98 SP. **Benedick:** See longer note, page 201.
98. **would:** wish
100. **ill:** bad
108. **clerk:** i.e., parish clerk, who led the responses during church services
112. **At a word:** i.e., in short, briefly
116. **dry hand:** supposedly a sign of age or sickness

PRINCE   And when please you to say so?
HERO   When I like your favor, for God defend the lute
  should be like the case.
PRINCE   My visor is Philemon's roof; within the house
  is Jove.   95
HERO   Why, then, your visor should be thatched.
PRINCE   Speak low if you speak love.
                          ⌈*They move aside;*
               Benedick and Margaret move forward.⌉
BENEDICK, ⌈*to Margaret*⌉   Well, I would you did like me.
MARGARET   So would not I for your own sake, for I have
  many ill qualities.   100
BENEDICK   Which is one?
MARGARET   I say my prayers aloud.
BENEDICK   I love you the better; the hearers may cry
  "Amen."
MARGARET   God match me with a good dancer.   105
                   ⌈*They separate; Benedick moves aside;*
                          Balthasar moves forward.⌉
BALTHASAR   Amen.
MARGARET   And God keep him out of my sight when the
  dance is done. Answer, clerk.
BALTHASAR   No more words. The clerk is answered.
                          ⌈*They move aside;*
               Ursula and Antonio move forward.⌉
URSULA   I know you well enough. You are Signior   110
  Antonio.
ANTONIO   At a word, I am not.
URSULA   I know you by the waggling of your head.
ANTONIO   To tell you true, I counterfeit him.
URSULA   You could never do him so ill-well unless you   115
  were the very man. Here's his dry hand up and
  down. You are he, you are he.
ANTONIO   At a word, I am not.
URSULA   Come, come, do you think I do not know you
  by your excellent wit? Can virtue hide itself? Go to,   120

121. **mum:** i.e., hush; **Graces:** virtues

121–22. **there's an end:** i.e., that's all there is to it

128. **The Hundred Merry Tales:** a popular joke book

135. **jester:** i.e., professional fool, who makes his living by entertaining his aristocratic patron

136. **only his gift:** i.e., his only talent

141. **fleet:** i.e., company of maskers; **boarded:** i.e., accosted, spoken to (literally, come alongside or aboard)

144. **break a comparison:** i.e., hit me with figures of speech as if they were lances in a joust

145. **peradventure not marked:** i.e., if it is perhaps not noted

151. **ill:** bad (thing)

From *A hundred merry tales* (1526; 1887 facs.).

mum, you are he. Graces will appear, and there's an
end.

⌜*They move aside;*
Benedick and Beatrice move forward.⌝

BEATRICE   Will you not tell me who told you so?

BENEDICK   No, you shall pardon me.

BEATRICE   Nor will you not tell me who you are?   125

BENEDICK   Not now.

BEATRICE   That I was disdainful, and that I had my
good wit out of *The Hundred Merry Tales*! Well, this
was Signior Benedick that said so.

BENEDICK   What's he?   130

BEATRICE   I am sure you know him well enough.

BENEDICK   Not I, believe me.

BEATRICE   Did he never make you laugh?

BENEDICK   I pray you, what is he?

BEATRICE   Why, he is the Prince's jester, a very dull   135
fool; only his gift is in devising impossible slanders.
None but libertines delight in him, and the com-
mendation is not in his wit but in his villainy, for he
both pleases men and angers them, and then they
laugh at him and beat him. I am sure he is in the   140
fleet. I would he had boarded me.

BENEDICK   When I know the gentleman, I'll tell him
what you say.

BEATRICE   Do, do. He'll but break a comparison or two
on me, which peradventure not marked or not   145
laughed at strikes him into melancholy, and then
there's a partridge wing saved, for the fool will eat
no supper that night. ⌜*Music for the dance.*⌝ We must
follow the leaders.

BENEDICK   In every good thing.   150

BEATRICE   Nay, if they lead to any ill, I will leave them
at the next turning.

Dance. ⌜*Then*⌝ *exit* ⌜*all except*
Don John, Borachio, and Claudio.⌝

153. **Sure:** i.e., surely
154–55. **break with:** i.e., speak to, reveal his thoughts to
163. **birth:** inherited social rank
169. **the banquet:** i.e., dessert and wine
171. **these ill news:** i.e., this bad news
174. **Save:** except; **office:** duties, functions; **affairs:** pursuits
175. **Therefore all:** i.e., therefore, let all
178. **faith:** faithfulness, loyalty; **blood:** i.e., sensual appetite, passion
179. **accident:** occurrence, happening; **of hourly proof:** i.e., demonstrated every hour
180. **mistrusted not:** did not suspect or anticipate

Winding a recheat. (1.1.236–37)
From T[homas] F[ella],
A book of diverse devices . . . (1585–98, 1622).

DON JOHN, ⌜*to Borachio*⌝ Sure my brother is amorous
    on Hero, and hath withdrawn her father to break
    with him about it. The ladies follow her, and but one   155
    visor remains.
BORACHIO And that is Claudio. I know him by his
    bearing.
DON JOHN, ⌜*to Claudio*⌝ Are not you Signior Benedick?
CLAUDIO You know me well. I am he.   160
DON JOHN Signior, you are very near my brother in his
    love. He is enamored on Hero. I pray you dissuade
    him from her. She is no equal for his birth. You
    may do the part of an honest man in it.
CLAUDIO How know you he loves her?   165
DON JOHN I heard him swear his affection.
BORACHIO So did I too, and he swore he would marry
    her tonight.
DON JOHN Come, let us to the banquet.
                              They exit. Claudio remains.
CLAUDIO, ⌜*unmasking*⌝
    Thus answer I in name of Benedick,   170
    But hear these ill news with the ears of Claudio.
    'Tis certain so, the Prince woos for himself.
    Friendship is constant in all other things
    Save in the office and affairs of love.
    Therefore all hearts in love use their own tongues.   175
    Let every eye negotiate for itself
    And trust no agent, for beauty is a witch
    Against whose charms faith melteth into blood.
    This is an accident of hourly proof,
    Which I mistrusted not. Farewell therefore, Hero.   180

                    Enter Benedick.

BENEDICK Count Claudio?
CLAUDIO Yea, the same.
BENEDICK Come, will you go with me?
CLAUDIO Whither?

185. **willow:** Willow garlands signified the grief of unrequited or lost love. (See page 70.)

186. **county:** i.e., count

186–87. **What . . . of:** i.e., in what fashion will you wear the garland?

189. **one way:** i.e., one way or the other

192–93. **so . . . bullocks:** i.e., cattle drivers (**drovers**) use such language when selling their oxen (See page 150.)

194. **served:** treated

196–98. **now . . . post:** i.e., you are hitting out blindly, striking the messenger (**post**) rather than the thief (See longer note, page 201.)

199. **If . . . be:** i.e., if you will not leave me

203–4. **but so:** perhaps, but in being merry; or, perhaps, in allowing myself to believe that "I go under that title"

205. **base:** unworthy, despicable

206. **puts . . . person:** i.e., thinks the whole world sees me as she does

206–7. **so gives me out:** describes me that way

210. **Troth:** i.e., in troth, in faith (a mild oath)

211. **Lady Fame: Fame** (or Rumor) was sometimes personified as a woman. (See page 78.)

212. **lodge:** perhaps, a solitary house; **warren:** an enclosed game preserve (There is disagreement about what this phrase might mean.)

216. **rod:** i.e., a bundle of willow switches

BENEDICK   Even to the next willow, about your own 185
  business, county. What fashion will you wear the
  garland of? About your neck like an usurer's chain?
  Or under your arm like a lieutenant's scarf? You
  must wear it one way, for the Prince hath got your
  Hero.   190
CLAUDIO   I wish him joy of her.
BENEDICK   Why, that's spoken like an honest drover; so
  they sell bullocks. But did you think the Prince
  would have served you thus?
CLAUDIO   I pray you, leave me.   195
BENEDICK   Ho, now you strike like the blind man.
  'Twas the boy that stole your meat, and you'll beat
  the post.
CLAUDIO   If it will not be, I'll leave you.   *He exits.*
BENEDICK   Alas, poor hurt fowl, now will he creep into 200
  sedges. But that my Lady Beatrice should know
  me, and not know me! The Prince's fool! Ha, it may
  be I go under that title because I am merry. Yea, but
  so I am apt to do myself wrong. I am not so reputed!
  It is the base, though bitter, disposition of Beatrice 205
  that puts the world into her person and so gives me
  out. Well, I'll be revenged as I may.

  Enter the Prince, Hero, ⌜and⌝ Leonato.

PRINCE   Now, signior, where's the Count? Did you see
  him?
BENEDICK   Troth, my lord, I have played the part of 210
  Lady Fame. I found him here as melancholy as a
  lodge in a warren. I told him, and I think I told him
  true, that your Grace had got the goodwill of this
  young lady, and I offered him my company to a
  willow tree, either to make him a garland, as being 215
  forsaken, or to bind him up a rod, as being worthy to
  be whipped.
PRINCE   To be whipped? What's his fault?

219. **flat:** downright
220. **shows it:** i.e., shows it to
222. **a trust:** i.e., trusting someone
229. **them:** i.e., the birds in the nest
231. **If . . . saying:** i.e., if Hero's "song" is in accord with what you say
233. **to:** i.e., with
235. **wronged:** slandered
239. **scold:** quarrel
241. **a great thaw:** perhaps, a time when muddy roads would make travel impossible and life therefore dull; **huddling:** piling up
242. **conveyance:** dexterity
243. **mark:** archery or musket target
246. **terminations:** perhaps, terms or expressions (literally, the grammatical endings of words)
247. **to . . . Star:** i.e., everything as far as the North Star
248. **though . . . endowed with:** i.e., even if she possessed
250. **Hercules:** in Greek mythology, a hero of extraordinary strength and courage; **turned spit:** i.e., turn the roasting spit (See longer note, page 201.)
251. **his club:** Hercules is generally pictured wielding or leaning on a mighty **club,** which he uses as a weapon. (See page 146.)
252. **Ate:** Greek goddess of discord (pronounced Ah-tay)
252–56. **I would . . . thither:** i.e., I devoutly wish she would be conjured back into hell, since her presence on earth makes hell, where she belongs, a place of tranquillity and makes earth a place of discord **scholar:** i.e., someone who knows how to address evil spirits **conjure:** i.e., exorcise **thither:** i.e., to hell   *50*

BENEDICK   The flat transgression of a schoolboy who,
   being overjoyed with finding a bird's nest, shows it   220
   his companion, and he steals it.
PRINCE   Wilt thou make a trust a transgression? The
   transgression is in the stealer.
BENEDICK   Yet it had not been amiss the rod had been
   made, and the garland too, for the garland he   225
   might have worn himself, and the rod he might
   have bestowed on you, who, as I take it, have stolen
   his bird's nest.
PRINCE   I will but teach them to sing and restore them
   to the owner.   230
BENEDICK   If their singing answer your saying, by my
   faith, you say honestly.
PRINCE   The Lady Beatrice hath a quarrel to you. The
   gentleman that danced with her told her she is
   much wronged by you.   235
BENEDICK   O, she misused me past the endurance of a
   block! An oak but with one green leaf on it would
   have answered her. My very visor began to assume
   life and scold with her. She told me, not thinking I
   had been myself, that I was the Prince's jester, that I   240
   was duller than a great thaw, huddling jest upon jest
   with such impossible conveyance upon me that I
   stood like a man at a mark with a whole army
   shooting at me. She speaks poniards, and every
   word stabs. If her breath were as terrible as her   245
   terminations, there were no living near her; she
   would infect to the North Star. I would not marry
   her though she were endowed with all that Adam
   had left him before he transgressed. She would have
   made Hercules have turned spit, yea, and have cleft   250
   his club to make the fire, too. Come, talk not of her.
   You shall find her the infernal Ate in good apparel. I
   would to God some scholar would conjure her, for
   certainly, while she is here, a man may live as quiet

261. **Antipodes:** the region on the opposite side of the globe (See page 162.)

262. **toothpicker:** i.e., toothpick (usually a pointed quill, but sometimes made of gold or silver)

263–64. **Prester John:** in legend, a priest and monarch of a vast empire in Asia or Africa

264. **great Cham:** i.e., Kublai Khan, Mongol emperor of China

265. **Pygmies:** in legend, a race of very small people living in Ethiopia or India

266. **harpy:** sharp-tongued woman; monstrous mythological creature with the face and breasts of a woman and the wings and talons of a bird

273–77. **Indeed . . . lost it:** These enigmatic lines suggest a past love relationship between Benedick and Beatrice. **gave him use:** i.e., paid him interest

278. **put . . . down:** humiliated; defeated (Beatrice, in her reply, gives the words a literal, sexual, meaning.)

283. **wherefore:** why

A harpy. (2.1.266)
From Conrad Lycosthenes, *Prodigiorum* . . . (1557).

in hell as in a sanctuary, and people sin upon 255
purpose because they would go thither. So indeed
all disquiet, horror, and perturbation follows her.

Enter Claudio and Beatrice.

PRINCE   Look, here she comes.

BENEDICK   Will your Grace command me any service
to the world's end? I will go on the slightest errand 260
now to the Antipodes that you can devise to send
me on. I will fetch you a toothpicker now from the
furthest inch of Asia, bring you the length of Prester
John's foot, fetch you a hair off the great Cham's
beard, do you any embassage to the Pygmies, rather 265
than hold three words' conference with this harpy.
You have no employment for me?

PRINCE   None but to desire your good company.

BENEDICK   O God, sir, here's a dish I love not! I cannot
endure my Lady Tongue.   *He exits.*   270

PRINCE, ⌜*to Beatrice*⌝   Come, lady, come, you have lost
the heart of Signior Benedick.

BEATRICE   Indeed, my lord, he lent it me awhile, and I
gave him use for it, a double heart for his single
one. Marry, once before he won it of me with false 275
dice. Therefore your Grace may well say I have lost
it.

PRINCE   You have put him down, lady, you have put
him down.

BEATRICE   So I would not he should do me, my lord, 280
lest I should prove the mother of fools. I have
brought Count Claudio, whom you sent me to seek.

PRINCE   Why, how now, count, wherefore are you sad?

CLAUDIO   Not sad, my lord.

PRINCE   How then, sick?   285

CLAUDIO   Neither, my lord.

BEATRICE   The Count is neither sad, nor sick, nor mer-

288. **civil as an orange:** i.e., like a Seville orange, described as "between sweet and sour"

289. **something . . . complexion:** i.e., he is jealous (The **complexion** of the orange is close to yellow, a color associated with jealousy.)

290. **blazon . . . true:** description . . . accurate

291. **conceit:** notion, idea

293. **broke with:** i.e., broached (the subject) with

298. **all grace:** perhaps, may God Himself

307–8. **on the windy side of:** i.e., out of reach of   **windy:** windward

311. **alliance:** marriage

311–12. **goes everyone to the world:** i.e., everyone gets married (a common idiom)

312. **sunburnt:** perhaps, dark-skinned (and hence unattractive, in Elizabethan eyes); or, perhaps, unprotected by marriage and thus open to the rough effects of wind and sun

313. **Heigh-ho for a husband:** proverbial (and also the title of a ballad)

316. **getting:** begetting

317. **got:** begot

318. **come by:** acquire

321. **costly:** valuable

323. **no matter:** i.e., nothing of significance or substance

ry, nor well, but civil count, civil as an orange, and
something of that jealous complexion.

PRINCE   I' faith, lady, I think your blazon to be true,   290
though I'll be sworn, if he be so, his conceit is
false.—Here, Claudio, I have wooed in thy name,
and fair Hero is won. I have broke with her father
and his goodwill obtained. Name the day of marriage, and God give thee joy.   295

LEONATO   Count, take of me my daughter, and with her
my fortunes. His Grace hath made the match, and
all grace say "Amen" to it.

BEATRICE   Speak, count, 'tis your cue.

CLAUDIO   Silence is the perfectest herald of joy. I were   300
but little happy if I could say how much.—Lady, as
you are mine, I am yours. I give away myself for you
and dote upon the exchange.

BEATRICE   Speak, cousin, or, if you cannot, stop his
mouth with a kiss and let not him speak neither.   305

PRINCE   In faith, lady, you have a merry heart.

BEATRICE   Yea, my lord. I thank it, poor fool, it keeps on
the windy side of care. My cousin tells him in his ear
that he is in her heart.

CLAUDIO   And so she doth, cousin.   310

BEATRICE   Good Lord for alliance! Thus goes everyone
to the world but I, and I am sunburnt. I may sit in a
corner and cry "Heigh-ho for a husband!"

PRINCE   Lady Beatrice, I will get you one.

BEATRICE   I would rather have one of your father's   315
getting. Hath your Grace ne'er a brother like you?
Your father got excellent husbands, if a maid could
come by them.

PRINCE   Will you have me, lady?

BEATRICE   No, my lord, unless I might have another for   320
working days. Your Grace is too costly to wear
every day. But I beseech your Grace pardon me. I
was born to speak all mirth and no matter.

325. **out o' question:** i.e., beyond dispute

332–33. **I cry . . . pardon:** Beatrice apologizes to Leonato and excuses herself from Don Pedro's presence

342. **out of suit:** i.e., out of wooing her

343. **were:** i.e., would be

346–47. **go to church:** i.e., get married

349. **his:** i.e., its

351. **a just sevennight:** i.e., exactly a week

352. **answer my mind:** i.e., correspond to my wishes

354. **breathing:** i.e., pause (literally, a time to breathe or rest); **warrant:** promise

356. **Hercules' labors:** Hercules was forced to perform twelve impossible tasks. (See note to line 250.)

359. **fain:** gladly

"Time goes on crutches." (2.1.348)
From Francesco Petrarca, *Opera* . . . (1508).

PRINCE   Your silence most offends me, and to be merry
best becomes you, for out o' question you were   325
born in a merry hour.

BEATRICE   No, sure, my lord, my mother cried, but then
there was a star danced, and under that was I
born.—Cousins, God give you joy!

LEONATO   Niece, will you look to those things I told   330
you of?

BEATRICE   I cry you mercy, uncle.—By your Grace's
pardon.   *Beatrice exits.*

PRINCE   By my troth, a pleasant-spirited lady.

LEONATO   There's little of the melancholy element in   335
her, my lord. She is never sad but when she sleeps,
and not ever sad then, for I have heard my daughter
say she hath often dreamt of unhappiness and
waked herself with laughing.

PRINCE   She cannot endure to hear tell of a husband.   340

LEONATO   O, by no means. She mocks all her wooers
out of suit.

PRINCE   She were an excellent wife for Benedick.

LEONATO   O Lord, my lord, if they were but a week
married, they would talk themselves mad.   345

PRINCE   County Claudio, when mean you to go to
church?

CLAUDIO   Tomorrow, my lord. Time goes on crutches
till love have all his rites.

LEONATO   Not till Monday, my dear son, which is hence   350
a just sevennight, and a time too brief, too, to have
all things answer my mind.

PRINCE, ⌜*to Claudio*⌝   Come, you shake the head at so
long a breathing, but I warrant thee, Claudio, the
time shall not go dully by us. I will in the interim   355
undertake one of Hercules' labors, which is to bring
Signior Benedick and the Lady Beatrice into a
mountain of affection, th' one with th' other. I
would fain have it a match, and I doubt not but to

360. **fashion:** contrive, manage; **minister:** provide
362. **I am for you:** i.e., I support you
362–63. **ten nights' watchings:** i.e., ten nights without sleep
366. **do . . . office:** play any small (or, perhaps, tasteful, suitable) part
368. **unhopefullest:** most unpromising
370. **strain:** birth; **approved:** demonstrated
372. **that:** i.e., so that
373. **practice on:** play a trick on, deceive
375. **queasy stomach:** i.e., distaste (for marriage)
376. **Cupid . . . archer:** See note to 1.1.39.
378. **drift:** scheme, plan

2.2 Don John and his henchman Borachio agree on a plan to disrupt the coming marriage: Borachio will convince Claudio that Hero is unfaithful by staging a meeting with Margaret, Hero's waiting gentlewoman. Margaret will be dressed in Hero's clothes, and Claudio will think that Borachio is Hero's lover.

---

3. **cross:** impede, block
4. **bar:** barrier; **cross:** trouble, misfortune, annoyance
5. **med'cinable:** medicinal, healing
6–7. **ranges evenly with:** i.e., goes in the same direction as

fashion it, if you three will but minister such   360
assistance as I shall give you direction.
LEONATO   My lord, I am for you, though it cost me ten
nights' watchings.
CLAUDIO   And I, my lord.
PRINCE   And you too, gentle Hero?   365
HERO   I will do any modest office, my lord, to help my
cousin to a good husband.
PRINCE   And Benedick is not the unhopefullest husband that I know. Thus far can I praise him: he is of
a noble strain, of approved valor, and confirmed   370
honesty. I will teach you how to humor your
cousin that she shall fall in love with Benedick.—
And I, with your two helps, will so practice on
Benedick that, in despite of his quick wit and his
queasy stomach, he shall fall in love with Beatrice.   375
If we can do this, Cupid is no longer an archer; his
glory shall be ours, for we are the only love gods. Go
in with me, and I will tell you my drift.

⌜*They*⌝ *exit.*

⌜Scene 2⌝
Enter ⌜*Don*⌝ *John and Borachio.*

DON JOHN   It is so. The Count Claudio shall marry the
daughter of Leonato.
BORACHIO   Yea, my lord, but I can cross it.
DON JOHN   Any bar, any cross, any impediment will be
med'cinable to me. I am sick in displeasure to him,   5
and whatsoever comes athwart his affection ranges
evenly with mine. How canst thou cross this marriage?
BORACHIO   Not honestly, my lord, but so covertly that
no dishonesty shall appear in me.   10
DON JOHN   Show me briefly how.

12. **since:** ago
13. **in the favor of:** i.e., in favor with, in the good graces of
14. **waiting gentlewoman:** See note to 2.1.35.
16. **unseasonable:** unsuitable, unseemly
17. **appoint her:** make an appointment with her
17-18. **her lady's chamber window:** i.e., the window of Hero's private quarters, perhaps her bedroom
21. **temper:** compound, produce by mixing ingredients
22. **spare not to tell:** i.e., go so far as to tell **spare:** refrain
25. **hold up:** support; **stale:** low-class harlot or prostitute
28. **misuse:** abuse
29. **undo:** destroy
30. **issue:** result
31. **despite:** spite, torment
33. **meet:** suitable
35. **intend:** pretend, claim
36. **as in love of:** i.e., as if because of your concern for
38. **like:** likely; **cozened:** tricked, cheated
41. **trial:** i.e., putting it to the test; **instances:** evidence
43. **term:** call
44. **Claudio:** Some editors substitute the word "Borachio" here. See longer note, page 202.
46. **fashion:** contrive, cleverly plan

BORACHIO   I think I told your Lordship a year since, how much I am in the favor of Margaret, the waiting gentlewoman to Hero.

DON JOHN   I remember.   15

BORACHIO   I can, at any unseasonable instant of the night, appoint her to look out at her lady's chamber window.

DON JOHN   What life is in that to be the death of this marriage?   20

BORACHIO   The poison of that lies in you to temper. Go you to the Prince your brother; spare not to tell him that he hath wronged his honor in marrying the renowned Claudio, whose estimation do you mightily hold up, to a contaminated stale, such a   25 one as Hero.

DON JOHN   What proof shall I make of that?

BORACHIO   Proof enough to misuse the Prince, to vex Claudio, to undo Hero, and kill Leonato. Look you for any other issue?   30

DON JOHN   Only to despite them I will endeavor anything.

BORACHIO   Go then, find me a meet hour to draw Don Pedro and the Count Claudio alone. Tell them that you know that Hero loves me; intend a kind of zeal   35 both to the Prince and Claudio, as in love of your brother's honor, who hath made this match, and his friend's reputation, who is thus like to be cozened with the semblance of a maid, that you have discovered thus. They will scarcely believe this without   40 trial. Offer them instances, which shall bear no less likelihood than to see me at her chamber window, hear me call Margaret "Hero," hear Margaret term me "Claudio," and bring them to see this the very night before the intended wedding, for in the mean-   45 time I will so fashion the matter that Hero shall be absent, and there shall appear such seeming truth

48. **disloyalty:** unfaithfulness; **jealousy:** suspicion, distrust

49. **assurance:** certainty; **preparation:** i.e., for the wedding

50. **issue:** result

52. **ducats:** gold coins

53. **constant:** steadfast, firm

55. **presently:** at once

2.3 Leonato, Claudio, and Don Pedro stage a conversation for Benedick to overhear. They talk about Beatrice's desperate love for Benedick, about their fears that her suffering will destroy her, and about how Benedick would mock Beatrice if he knew of her love. Benedick decides that he must love Beatrice in return.

---

4. **orchard:** formal garden (See page 74.)

5. **I am here already:** i.e., I will return immediately (Benedick pretends that the words have their literal meaning.)

11. **argument:** subject, theme

14. **drum, fife:** i.e., military music (See page 215.)

15. **tabor:** small drum, used with a tabor-**pipe** to accompany dancing (See page 102.)

17. **armor:** i.e., suit of armor

18. **carving:** i.e., planning; **doublet:** close-fitting jacket

18–19. **was wont to:** i.e., used to

19. **plain:** i.e., simply, straightforwardly

of Hero's disloyalty that jealousy shall be called
assurance and all the preparation overthrown.

DON JOHN   Grow this to what adverse issue it can, I will   50
put it in practice. Be cunning in the working this,
and thy fee is a thousand ducats.

BORACHIO   Be you constant in the accusation, and my
cunning shall not shame me.

DON JOHN   I will presently go learn their day of mar-   55
riage.

⌐*They*⌐ *exit.*

⌐Scene 3⌐
Enter Benedick alone.

BENEDICK   Boy!

⌐*Enter Boy.*⌐

BOY   Signior?

BENEDICK   In my chamber window lies a book. Bring it
hither to me in the orchard.

BOY   I am here already, sir.   5

BENEDICK   I know that, but I would have thee hence
and here again.   ⌐*Boy*⌐ *exits.*
I do much wonder that one man, seeing how much
another man is a fool when he dedicates his behaviors to love, will, after he hath laughed at such   10
shallow follies in others, become the argument of
his own scorn by falling in love—and such a man is
Claudio. I have known when there was no music
with him but the drum and the fife, and now had he
rather hear the tabor and the pipe; I have known   15
when he would have walked ten mile afoot to see a
good armor, and now will he lie ten nights awake
carving the fashion of a new doublet. He was wont
to speak plain and to the purpose, like an honest

20–21. **turned orthography:** i.e., become a fancy speaker (**Orthography** is, literally, the study of proper spelling.)

27. **fair:** beautiful; **well:** i.e., healthy (not "sick" with love)

29. **graces:** pleasing qualities

30. **grace:** favor

31. **I'll none:** i.e., I'll not have her; **cheapen:** bid for

32. **look on:** observe

33. **noble, angel:** In addition to their normal meanings, these words were also the names of coins.

34. **discourse:** i.e., ability to converse

39. **harmony:** music, pleasing sounds

41. **The music ended:** i.e., when the music has ended

42. **fit . . . pennyworth:** This much-debated phrase links Benedick to the **kid-fox** (perhaps, a young fox) and to some form of punishment. "To get one's **pennyworth** on" is "to take revenge on"; **pennyworth** also meant "a reward" or "a bargain." (Some editors print "hid-fox," since Benedick is hiding.)

44. **tax:** order, challenge

The Ponyard.

A poniard. (2.1.244)
From Louis de Gaya,
A treatise of the arms . . . (1678).

man and a soldier, and now is he turned orthogra-   20
phy; his words are a very fantastical banquet, just so
many strange dishes. May I be so converted and see
with these eyes? I cannot tell; I think not. I will not
be sworn but love may transform me to an oyster,
but I'll take my oath on it, till he have made an   25
oyster of me, he shall never make me such a fool.
One woman is fair, yet I am well; another is wise, yet
I am well; another virtuous, yet I am well; but till all
graces be in one woman, one woman shall not
come in my grace. Rich she shall be, that's certain;   30
wise, or I'll none; virtuous, or I'll never cheapen
her; fair, or I'll never look on her; mild, or come not
near me; noble, or not I for an angel; of good
discourse, an excellent musician, and her hair shall
be of what color it please God. Ha! The Prince and   35
Monsieur Love! I will hide me in the arbor.

⌈*He hides.*⌉

Enter Prince, Leonato, Claudio, and Balthasar
with music.

PRINCE   Come, shall we hear this music?
CLAUDIO
Yea, my good lord. How still the evening is,
As hushed on purpose to grace harmony!
PRINCE, ⌈*aside to Claudio*⌉
See you where Benedick hath hid himself?   40
CLAUDIO, ⌈*aside to Prince*⌉
O, very well, my lord. The music ended,
We'll fit the kid-fox with a pennyworth.
PRINCE
Come, Balthasar, we'll hear that song again.
BALTHASAR
O, good my lord, tax not so bad a voice
To slander music any more than once.   45

46. **witness:** sign, token; **still:** always

47. **put a strange face:** perhaps, pretend not to know; **his:** its

48. **let me woo:** i.e., make me entreat

50–52. **Since . . . loves:** Balthasar compares Don Pedro to a man who courts a woman whom he knows is unworthy.

55. **notes:** i.e., music

56. **Note:** take notice of

58. **crotchets:** (1) peculiar ideas; (2) quarter notes in music

59. **nothing:** There is some evidence that "nothing" and "noting" were pronounced alike in Shakespeare's day. If so, this word is yet another pun on "noting," and the title of the play itself could be heard as "Much Ado about Noting."

60. **air:** melody

61. **sheeps' guts:** used to make strings for lutes and other musical instruments (See page 122.)

62. **hale:** pull, draw

67. **constant:** faithful

69. **bonny:** smiling, bright

72. **mo:** i.e., more

73. **dumps:** (1) fits of melancholy or depression; (2) mournful songs; **dull:** gloomy; **heavy:** sad

75. **leavy:** filled with leaves

PRINCE
　It is the witness still of excellency
　To put a strange face on his own perfection.
　I pray thee, sing, and let me woo no more.
BALTHASAR
　Because you talk of wooing, I will sing,
　Since many a wooer doth commence his suit　　　　50
　To her he thinks not worthy, yet he woos,
　Yet will he swear he loves.
PRINCE　　　　　　　　　　Nay, pray thee, come,
　Or if thou wilt hold longer argument,
　Do it in notes.　　　　　　　　　　　　　　　55
BALTHASAR　　　Note this before my notes:
　There's not a note of mine that's worth the noting.
PRINCE
　Why, these are very crotchets that he speaks!
　Note notes, forsooth, and nothing.　　⌜*Music plays.*⌝
BENEDICK, ⌜*aside*⌝ Now, divine air! Now is his soul　60
　ravished. Is it not strange that sheeps' guts should
　hale souls out of men's bodies? Well, a horn for my
　money, when all's done.
⌜BALTHASAR *sings*⌝
　　　Sigh no more, ladies, sigh no more,
　　　　Men were deceivers ever,　　　　　　　　65
　　　One foot in sea and one on shore,
　　　　To one thing constant never.
　　　Then sigh not so, but let them go,
　　　　And be you blithe and bonny,
　　　Converting all your sounds of woe　　　　70
　　　　Into Hey, nonny nonny.

　　　Sing no more ditties, sing no mo,
　　　　Of dumps so dull and heavy.
　　　The fraud of men was ever so,
　　　　Since summer first was leavy.　　　　75

81. **an ill:** i.e., a bad

82. **faith:** a mild oath

82–83. **for a shift:** i.e., as a makeshift, for lack of something better

86. **bode no mischief:** i.e., does not prophesy misfortune

86–87. **had as lief:** i.e., would just as gladly

98. **Stalk on:** i.e., pursue our prey stealthily

99. **sits:** i.e., is roosting or perching (and thus easily caught)

105–6. **Sits . . . corner?:** i.e., does the wind blow from that direction?

109. **the infinite of:** i.e., the range of

110. **counterfeit:** pretend

111. **like enough:** i.e., that is likely

"In time the savage bull doth
bear the yoke." (1.1.256)
From Philip Ayres, *Emblemata amatoria* . . . (1683).

Then sigh not so, but let them go,
   And be you blithe and bonny,
Converting all your sounds of woe
   Into Hey, nonny nonny.

PRINCE   By my troth, a good song.   80
BALTHASAR   And an ill singer, my lord.
PRINCE   Ha, no, no, faith, thou sing'st well enough for a
   shift.
BENEDICK, ⌜*aside*⌝ An he had been a dog that should
   have howled thus, they would have hanged him. And   85
   I pray God his bad voice bode no mischief. I had as
   lief have heard the night raven, come what plague
   could have come after it.
PRINCE   Yea, marry, dost thou hear, Balthasar? I pray
   thee get us some excellent music, for tomorrow   90
   night we would have it at the Lady Hero's chamber
   window.
BALTHASAR   The best I can, my lord.
PRINCE   Do so. Farewell.   *Balthasar exits.*
   Come hither, Leonato. What was it you told me of   95
   today, that your niece Beatrice was in love with
   Signior Benedick?
CLAUDIO   O, ay. ⌜*Aside to Prince.*⌝ Stalk on, stalk on; the
   fowl sits.—I did never think that lady would have
   loved any man.   100
LEONATO   No, nor I neither, but most wonderful that
   she should so dote on Signior Benedick, whom she
   hath in all outward behaviors seemed ever to
   abhor.
BENEDICK, ⌜*aside*⌝ Is 't possible? Sits the wind in that   105
   corner?
LEONATO   By my troth, my lord, I cannot tell what to
   think of it, but that she loves him with an enraged
   affection, it is past the infinite of thought.
PRINCE   Maybe she doth but counterfeit.   110
CLAUDIO   Faith, like enough.

114. **discovers:** reveals, shows
118. **sit you:** i.e., sit
126. **gull:** trick; **but:** except
128. **himself:** i.e., itself; **reverence:** a reverend or venerable person
129. **ta'en th' infection:** i.e., caught the disease (we are spreading) **ta'en:** taken
130. **Hold it up:** i.e., keep it up
136. **says she:** i.e., says Beatrice
140. **smock:** slip, chemise

A willow. (2.1.185)
From Henry Peacham, *Minerua Britanna* . . . (1612).

LEONATO   O God! Counterfeit? There was never counterfeit of passion came so near the life of passion as
she discovers it.
PRINCE   Why, what effects of passion shows she?   115
CLAUDIO, ⌐*aside to Leonato*⌐   Bait the hook well; this fish
will bite.
LEONATO   What effects, my lord? She will sit you—you
heard my daughter tell you how.
CLAUDIO   She did indeed.   120
PRINCE   How, how I pray you? You amaze me. I would
have thought her spirit had been invincible against
all assaults of affection.
LEONATO   I would have sworn it had, my lord, especial-
ly against Benedick.   125
BENEDICK, ⌐*aside*⌐   I should think this a gull but that the
white-bearded fellow speaks it. Knavery cannot,
sure, hide himself in such reverence.
CLAUDIO, ⌐*aside to Prince*⌐   He hath ta'en th' infection.
Hold it up.   130
PRINCE   Hath she made her affection known to Bene-
dick?
LEONATO   No, and swears she never will. That's her
torment.
CLAUDIO   'Tis true indeed, so your daughter says. "Shall   135
I," says she, "that have so oft encountered him with
scorn, write to him that I love him?"
LEONATO   This says she now when she is beginning to
write to him, for she'll be up twenty times a night,
and there will she sit in her smock till she have writ   140
a sheet of paper. My daughter tells us all.
CLAUDIO   Now you talk of a sheet of paper, I remember
a pretty jest your daughter told ⌐us of.⌐
LEONATO   O, when she had writ it and was reading it
over, she found "Benedick" and "Beatrice" be-   145
tween the sheet?
CLAUDIO   That.

148–49. **halfpence:** i.e., little pieces

150. **immodest:** forward, impudent; **flout:** mock, scoff at

158. **ecstasy:** frenzy, madness; **overborne her:** overcome her

159–60. **do . . . herself:** harm herself dangerously

162. **discover:** reveal

163. **sport:** joke, jest

165. **an alms:** a good deed

166. **out of:** i.e., beyond

170. **blood:** passion

174. **dotage:** excessive love

175. **daffed:** i.e., doffed, put aside; **respects:** considerations

175–76. **made . . . myself:** i.e., married her

179. **she says:** i.e., Beatrice says

182. **rather than she will bate:** i.e., before she will leave off

183. **crossness:** contrariness

LEONATO   O, she tore the letter into a thousand halfpence, railed at herself that she should be so
immodest to write to one that she knew would flout   150
her. "I measure him," says she, "by my own spirit,
for I should flout him if he writ to me, yea, though I
love him, I should."

CLAUDIO   Then down upon her knees she falls, weeps,
sobs, beats her heart, tears her hair, prays, curses: 155
"O sweet Benedick, God give me patience!"

LEONATO   She doth indeed, my daughter says so, and
the ecstasy hath so much overborne her that my
daughter is sometimes afeared she will do a desperate outrage to herself. It is very true.   160

PRINCE   It were good that Benedick knew of it by some
other, if she will not discover it.

CLAUDIO   To what end? He would make but a sport of it
and torment the poor lady worse.

PRINCE   An he should, it were an alms to hang him.   165
She's an excellent sweet lady, and, out of all suspicion, she is virtuous.

CLAUDIO   And she is exceeding wise.

PRINCE   In everything but in loving Benedick.

LEONATO   O, my lord, wisdom and blood combating in   170
so tender a body, we have ten proofs to one that
blood hath the victory. I am sorry for her, as I have
just cause, being her uncle and her guardian.

PRINCE   I would she had bestowed this dotage on me. I
would have daffed all other respects and made her   175
half myself. I pray you tell Benedick of it, and hear
what he will say.

LEONATO   Were it good, think you?

CLAUDIO   Hero thinks surely she will die, for she says
she will die if he love her not, and she will die ere   180
she make her love known, and she will die if he woo
her rather than she will bate one breath of her
accustomed crossness.

184. **make tender of:** i.e., offer

186. **contemptible:** contemptuous, scornful

187. **proper:** handsome; or, fine, respectable

188. **good outward happiness:** perhaps, an attractive appearance; or, perhaps, the appearance of suitability

193. **Hector:** a Trojan warrior noted for courage

194. **quarrels:** hostilities, violent altercations

201. **by:** i.e., to judge by; **large:** improper, licentious

209. **the while:** in the meanwhile

214–15. **trust my expectation:** i.e., believe that I can predict the future

218. **carry:** manage; **sport:** amusement, fun

An orchard. (1.2.10, 2.3.4, 3.1.5)
From Octavio Boldoni, *Theatrum temporaneum* . . . (1636).

PRINCE   She doth well. If she should make tender of
   her love, 'tis very possible he'll scorn it, for the man,   185
   as you know all, hath a contemptible spirit.
CLAUDIO   He is a very proper man.
PRINCE   He hath indeed a good outward happiness.
CLAUDIO   Before God, and in my mind, very wise. .
PRINCE   He doth indeed show some sparks that are like   190
   wit.
CLAUDIO   And I take him to be valiant.
PRINCE   As Hector, I assure you, and in the managing
   of quarrels you may say he is wise, for either he
   avoids them with great discretion or undertakes   195
   them with a most Christianlike fear.
LEONATO   If he do fear God, he must necessarily keep
   peace. If he break the peace, he ought to enter into
   a quarrel with fear and trembling.
PRINCE   And so will he do, for the man doth fear God,   200
   howsoever it seems not in him by some large jests
   he will make. Well, I am sorry for your niece. Shall
   we go seek Benedick and tell him of her love?
CLAUDIO   Never tell him, my lord, let her wear it out
   with good counsel.   205
LEONATO   Nay, that's impossible; she may wear her
   heart out first.
PRINCE   Well, we will hear further of it by your daughter. Let it cool the while. I love Benedick well, and I
   could wish he would modestly examine himself to   210
   see how much he is unworthy so good a lady.
LEONATO   My lord, will you walk? Dinner is ready.
      ⌜*Leonato, Prince, and Claudio begin to exit.*⌝
CLAUDIO, ⌜*aside to Prince and Leonato*⌝ If he do not
   dote on her upon this, I will never trust my expectation.   215
PRINCE, ⌜*aside to Leonato*⌝ Let there be the same net
   spread for her, and that must your daughter and her
   gentlewomen carry. The sport will be when they

219. **hold one an opinion of another's dotage:** i.e., each holds the opinion that the other is in love

221. **dumb show:** literally, a theatrical scene without speech

224. **conference:** conversation; **sadly borne:** seriously conducted

226. **have their full bent:** This phrase suggests a bow, in archery, bent to its limit.

232. **their detractions:** i.e., words pointing out their faults

232–33. **put . . . mending:** i.e., mend the faults

235. **reprove:** reject

238. **some odd quirks:** i.e., a few quibbles

241. **meat:** i.e., food

242. **sentences:** maxims, sayings

243. **awe:** constrain or restrain through fear

244. **career:** course; **humor:** inclination

Cupid with a bow at "full bent." (2.3.226)
From August Casimir Redel,
Apophtegmata symbolica . . . (n.d.).

hold one an opinion of another's dotage, and no
such matter. That's the scene that I would see,   220
which will be merely a dumb show. Let us send her
to call him in to dinner.
                      ⌜*Prince, Leonato, and Claudio exit.*⌝
BENEDICK, ⌜*coming forward*⌝ This can be no trick. The
conference was sadly borne; they have the truth of
this from Hero; they seem to pity the lady. It seems   225
her affections have their full bent. Love me? Why, it
must be requited! I hear how I am censured. They
say I will bear myself proudly if I perceive the love
come from her. They say, too, that she will rather
die than give any sign of affection. I did never think   230
to marry. I must not seem proud. Happy are they
that hear their detractions and can put them to
mending. They say the lady is fair; 'tis a truth, I can
bear them witness. And virtuous; 'tis so, I cannot
reprove it. And wise, but for loving me; by my troth,   235
it is no addition to her wit, nor no great argument of
her folly, for I will be horribly in love with her! I
may chance have some odd quirks and remnants of
wit broken on me because I have railed so long
against marriage, but doth not the appetite alter? A   240
man loves the meat in his youth that he cannot
endure in his age. Shall quips and sentences and
these paper bullets of the brain awe a man from the
career of his humor? No! The world must be peopled. When I said I would die a bachelor, I did not   245
think I should live till I were married. Here comes
Beatrice. By this day, she's a fair lady. I do spy some
marks of love in her.

Enter Beatrice.

BEATRICE Against my will, I am sent to bid you come
    in to dinner.   250
BENEDICK Fair Beatrice, I thank you for your pains.

257. **daw:** jackdaw, a small kind of crow

258. **stomach:** appetite

264. **pity of:** i.e., pity on

265. **Jew:** From the Middle Ages, when Jews were kept from almost all occupations except moneylending, the word "Jew" was sometimes used as a term of contempt for anyone who (like some moneylenders) was ungenerous or cruel.

"Lady Fame." (2.1.211)
From August Casimir Redel,
Apophtegmata symbolica . . . (n.d.).

BEATRICE   I took no more pains for those thanks than
you take pains to thank me. If it had been painful, I
would not have come.

BENEDICK   You take pleasure then in the message?   255

BEATRICE   Yea, just so much as you may take upon a
knife's point and choke a daw withal. You have no
stomach, signior. Fare you well.   *She exits.*

BENEDICK   Ha! "Against my will I am sent to bid you
come in to dinner." There's a double meaning in   260
that. "I took no more pains for those thanks than
you took pains to thank me." That's as much as to
say "Any pains that I take for you is as easy as
thanks." If I do not take pity of her, I am a villain; if I
do not love her, I am a Jew. I will go get her picture.   265
          He exits.

MUCH ADO
ABOUT NOTHING

ACT 3

3.1 Beatrice is lured into overhearing a staged conversation between Hero and Ursula, a waiting gentlewoman, who talk about Benedick's desperate love for Beatrice and about Beatrice's arrogance. Beatrice decides that she must return Benedick's love.

---

3. **Proposing:** talking
4. **Whisper her:** i.e., whisper in her
7. **pleachèd:** bordered with intertwined boughs (See page 223.)
9–10. **favorites . . . that advance:** i.e., especially indulged courtiers . . . who display or raise up
11. **bred it:** brought it forth
13. **listen our propose:** i.e., listen to our discussion; **office:** assigned part
14. **Bear thee:** i.e., conduct yourself
15. **warrant:** promise; **presently:** at once
17. **trace:** tread; **alley:** garden path

Honeysuckle or woodbine. (3.1.8, 3.1.31)
From John Gerard, *The herball* . . . (1597).

Enter Hero and two gentlewomen, Margaret and Ursula.

HERO

  Good Margaret, run thee to the parlor.
  There shalt thou find my cousin Beatrice
  Proposing with the Prince and Claudio.
  Whisper her ear and tell her I and Ursula
  Walk in the orchard, and our whole discourse   5
  Is all of her. Say that thou overheardst us,
  And bid her steal into the pleachèd bower
  Where honeysuckles ripened by the sun
  Forbid the sun to enter, like favorites
  Made proud by princes, that advance their pride   10
  Against that power that bred it. There will she hide
    her
  To listen our propose. This is thy office.
  Bear thee well in it, and leave us alone.

MARGARET

  I'll make her come, I warrant you, presently.   15
                           ┌*She exits.*┐

HERO

  Now, Ursula, when Beatrice doth come,
  As we do trace this alley up and down,
  Our talk must only be of Benedick.
  When I do name him, let it be thy part
  To praise him more than ever man did merit.   20

22. **matter:** i.e., material
23. **Cupid's . . . arrow:** See note to 1.1.39.
24. **only wounds by:** i.e., wounds by mere
26. **conference:** conversation
27–29. **The pleasant'st . . . bait:** i.e., the most pleasant moment in fishing is when the fish rushes to take the bait **her . . . oars:** i.e., its fins
31. **couchèd:** hidden; **woodbine coverture:** i.e., screen of honeysuckle (See page 82.)
32. **Fear you not:** i.e., don't worry about
36. **coy:** distant, disdainful; **wild:** rebellious, not submitting to control
37. **haggards:** wild female hawks; **rock:** cliff
44. **with affection:** i.e., with his emotions

A haggard falcon. (3.1.37)
From George Turberville, *The booke of faulconrie . . .* (1575).

My talk to thee must be how Benedick
Is sick in love with Beatrice. Of this matter
Is little Cupid's crafty arrow made,
That only wounds by hearsay. Now begin,
For look where Beatrice like a lapwing runs   25
Close by the ground, to hear our conference.

Enter Beatrice, ⌜*who hides in the bower.*⌝

URSULA, ⌜*aside to Hero*⌝
The pleasant'st angling is to see the fish
Cut with her golden oars the silver stream
And greedily devour the treacherous bait.
So angle we for Beatrice, who even now   30
Is couchèd in the woodbine coverture.
Fear you not my part of the dialogue.
HERO, ⌜*aside to Ursula*⌝
Then go we near her, that her ear lose nothing
Of the false sweet bait that we lay for it.—
                    ⌜*They walk near the bower.*⌝
No, truly, Ursula, she is too disdainful.   35
I know her spirits are as coy and wild
As haggards of the rock.
URSULA   But are you sure
That Benedick loves Beatrice so entirely?
HERO
So says the Prince and my new-trothèd lord.   40
URSULA
And did they bid you tell her of it, madam?
HERO
They did entreat me to acquaint her of it,
But I persuaded them, if they loved Benedick,
To wish him wrestle with affection
And never to let Beatrice know of it.   45
URSULA
Why did you so? Doth not the gentleman

47. **as full:** i.e., fully
48. **couch:** lie down
54. **wit:** cleverness; ability to speak sharply or amusingly
56. **All matter else seems weak:** i.e., all other conversation seems worthless
57. **project:** idea, notion
61. **make sport at:** i.e., mock, make fun of
63. **How:** i.e., no matter how; **rarely:** beautifully; **featured:** formed
64. **spell him backward:** i.e., describe him perversely; **fair-faced:** of a fair complexion; or, beautifully featured
67. **black:** i.e., dark-skinned; **of an antic:** i.e., a grotesque or fantastic figure
69. **low:** short; **an agate:** i.e., like a tiny figure carved on an agate-stone ring
70. **vane:** i.e., weather vane
71. **moved . . . none:** i.e., that cannot be moved by any wind, no matter how strong
74. **simpleness:** sincerity, integrity
75. **commendable:** pronounced **còmmendable**
76. **from all fashions:** unlike customary or accepted ways of behaving

    Deserve as full as fortunate a bed
    As ever Beatrice shall couch upon?
HERO
    O god of love! I know he doth deserve
    As much as may be yielded to a man,   50
    But Nature never framed a woman's heart
    Of prouder stuff than that of Beatrice.
    Disdain and scorn ride sparkling in her eyes,
    Misprizing what they look on, and her wit
    Values itself so highly that to her   55
    All matter else seems weak. She cannot love,
    Nor take no shape nor project of affection,
    She is so self-endeared.
URSULA   Sure, I think so,
    And therefore certainly it were not good   60
    She knew his love, lest she'll make sport at it.
HERO
    Why, you speak truth. I never yet saw man,
    How wise, how noble, young, how rarely featured,
    But she would spell him backward. If fair-faced,
    She would swear the gentleman should be her   65
      sister;
    If black, why, Nature, drawing of an antic,
    Made a foul blot; if tall, a lance ill-headed;
    If low, an agate very vilely cut;
    If speaking, why, a vane blown with all winds;   70
    If silent, why, a block moved with none.
    So turns she every man the wrong side out,
    And never gives to truth and virtue that
    Which simpleness and merit purchaseth.
URSULA
    Sure, sure, such carping is not commendable.   75
HERO
    No, not to be so odd and from all fashions
    As Beatrice is cannot be commendable.
    But who dare tell her so? If I should speak,

81. **press me to death:** an allusion to the torture of a prisoner by loading heavy weights on his chest until the prisoner dies

82. **covered fire:** Proverbial: "Fire that's closest kept burns most of all."

83. **Consume away, waste:** i.e., be destroyed (**Sighs** were thought to draw blood from the heart.)

89. **honest slanders:** perhaps, malicious statements that do not, however, attack her chastity (**Honest,** when applied to a woman, standardly meant "chaste.")

95. **prized to have:** esteemed as having; or, credited with having

97. **the only:** i.e., the very best

100. **Speaking my fancy:** i.e., for expressing my own preference

101. **argument:** ability to converse

103. **name:** reputation

105. **are you married:** i.e., will you be married

106. **every day, tomorrow:** i.e., after tomorrow (I'll be married) all the time

She would mock me into air. O, she would laugh
    me   80
Out of myself, press me to death with wit.
Therefore let Benedick, like covered fire,
Consume away in sighs, waste inwardly.
It were a better death than die with mocks,
Which is as bad as die with tickling.   85

URSULA
Yet tell her of it. Hear what she will say.

HERO
No, rather I will go to Benedick
And counsel him to fight against his passion;
And truly I'll devise some honest slanders
To stain my cousin with. One doth not know   90
How much an ill word may empoison liking.

URSULA
O, do not do your cousin such a wrong!
She cannot be so much without true judgment,
Having so swift and excellent a wit
As she is prized to have, as to refuse   95
So rare a gentleman as Signior Benedick.

HERO
He is the only man of Italy,
Always excepted my dear Claudio.

URSULA
I pray you be not angry with me, madam,
Speaking my fancy: Signior Benedick,   100
For shape, for bearing, argument, and valor,
Goes foremost in report through Italy.

HERO
Indeed, he hath an excellent good name.

URSULA
His excellence did earn it ere he had it.
When are you married, madam?   105

HERO
Why, every day, tomorrow. Come, go in.

107. **attires:** headdresses
109. **limed:** i.e., trapped like a bird in birdlime
111. **haps:** chance, accident
116. **such:** i.e., contemptuous and proud maidens
120. **band:** i.e., bond
122. **reportingly:** i.e., by report or hearsay

3.2 Benedick appears with his beard shaved off and showing other signs of having fallen in love. When he exits with Leonato, Don John tells Don Pedro and Claudio that Hero is unfaithful and that he will show them a man entering her chamber window that very night, the night before the wedding.

1–2. **consummate:** i.e., consummated, completed
3. **bring you thither:** i.e., go with you to Aragon
3–4. **vouchsafe:** allow
5. **soil in:** i.e., stain on
7–8. **be bold with:** i.e., take the liberty of asking

I'll show thee some attires and have thy counsel
Which is the best to furnish me tomorrow.
⌜*They move away from the bower.*⌝
URSULA, ⌜*aside to Hero*⌝
She's limed, I warrant you. We have caught her,
madam.   110
HERO, ⌜*aside to Ursula*⌝
If it prove so, then loving goes by haps;
Some Cupid kills with arrows, some with traps.
⌜*Hero and Ursula exit.*⌝
BEATRICE, ⌜*coming forward*⌝
What fire is in mine ears? Can this be true?
Stand I condemned for pride and scorn so much?
Contempt, farewell, and maiden pride, adieu!   115
No glory lives behind the back of such.
And Benedick, love on; I will requite thee,
Taming my wild heart to thy loving hand.
If thou dost love, my kindness shall incite thee
To bind our loves up in a holy band.   120
For others say thou dost deserve, and I
Believe it better than reportingly.
She exits.

⌜Scene 2⌝
Enter Prince, Claudio, Benedick, and Leonato.

PRINCE   I do but stay till your marriage be consummate, and then go I toward Aragon.
CLAUDIO   I'll bring you thither, my lord, if you'll vouchsafe me.
PRINCE   Nay, that would be as great a soil in the new   5
gloss of your marriage as to show a child his new
coat and forbid him to wear it. I will only be bold
with Benedick for his company, for from the crown
of his head to the sole of his foot he is all mirth. He

11. **hangman:** i.e., executioner, torturer (Cupid)

16. **Methinks:** it seems to me; **sadder:** more serious

18. **truant:** rogue; **true:** honest, sincere

20. **wants:** lacks

22. **Draw it:** i.e., pull (the tooth)

23. **Hang it:** an exclamation of impatience

24. **hang, draw:** Criminals were first hanged, then drawn (disemboweled).

26. **Where is but a humor or a worm:** In Elizabethan thinking, **toothache** was caused by humors (morbid secretions) descending from the head or rising from the stomach, or by worms invading the tooth.

27. **grief:** hurt, injury, suffering

30. **fancy:** love

31. **fancy:** whim, sudden liking (as also in line 36)

34. **slops:** wide baggy breeches or hose

37. **fool for fancy:** i.e., victim of love

42. **man:** i.e., servant

43. **the old ornament of his cheek:** i.e., his beard

hath twice or thrice cut Cupid's bowstring, and the   10
little hangman dare not shoot at him. He hath a
heart as sound as a bell, and his tongue is the
clapper, for what his heart thinks, his tongue
speaks.

BENEDICK   Gallants, I am not as I have been.   15

LEONATO   So say I. Methinks you are sadder.

CLAUDIO   I hope he be in love.

PRINCE   Hang him, truant! There's no true drop of
blood in him to be truly touched with love. If he be
sad, he wants money.   20

BENEDICK   I have the toothache.

PRINCE   Draw it.

BENEDICK   Hang it!

CLAUDIO   You must hang it first, and draw it afterwards.

PRINCE   What, sigh for the toothache?   25

LEONATO   Where is but a humor or a worm.

BENEDICK   Well, everyone ⌐can⌐ master a grief but he
that has it.

CLAUDIO   Yet say I, he is in love.

PRINCE   There is no appearance of fancy in him, unless   30
it be a fancy that he hath to strange disguises, as to
be a Dutchman today, a Frenchman tomorrow, or
in the shape of two countries at once, as a German
from the waist downward, all slops, and a Spaniard
from the hip upward, no doublet. Unless he have a   35
fancy to this foolery, as it appears he hath, he is no
fool for fancy, as you would have it appear he is.

CLAUDIO   If he be not in love with some woman, there
is no believing old signs. He brushes his hat o'
mornings. What should that bode?   40

PRINCE   Hath any man seen him at the barber's?

CLAUDIO   No, but the barber's man hath been seen
with him, and the old ornament of his cheek hath
already stuffed tennis balls.

47. **civet:** i.e., perfume

47-48. **smell him out:** i.e., discover his secret (with a pun on **smell**)

51. **note:** indication

53. **paint himself:** i.e., use cosmetics (**Wash his face,** line 52, may also have this meaning.); **the which:** i.e., his use of cosmetics

55-56. **crept . . . stops:** i.e., converted to love songs **stops:** the positions on the lute where the fingers are pressed to make particular sounds (with a pun on the **stops** or silences in his speech)

57. **heavy:** serious, grave

62. **ill conditions:** i.e., bad qualities

63. **dies:** wastes away (The Prince's response in line 64 plays on the Elizabethan use of the word *die* to allude to sexual orgasm.)

65. **charm for:** i.e., magic spell to cure

68. **hobby-horses:** i.e., jesters, buffoons

69. **For my life:** i.e., upon my life

70. **by this:** i.e., by this time

74. **e'en:** afternoon (literally, evening)

75. **If . . . served:** i.e., if you have the time

LEONATO   Indeed he looks younger than he did, by the   45
loss of a beard.
PRINCE   Nay, he rubs himself with civet. Can you smell
him out by that?
CLAUDIO   That's as much as to say, the sweet youth's in
love.   50
⌜PRINCE⌝   The greatest note of it is his melancholy.
CLAUDIO   And when was he wont to wash his face?
PRINCE   Yea, or to paint himself? For the which I hear
what they say of him.
CLAUDIO   Nay, but his jesting spirit, which is now crept   55
into a lute string and now governed by stops—
PRINCE   Indeed, that tells a heavy tale for him. Con-
clude, conclude, he is in love.
CLAUDIO   Nay, but I know who loves him.
PRINCE   That would I know, too. I warrant, one that   60
knows him not.
CLAUDIO   Yes, and his ill conditions; and, in despite of
all, dies for him.
PRINCE   She shall be buried with her face upwards.
BENEDICK   Yet is this no charm for the toothache.—   65
Old signior, walk aside with me. I have studied eight
or nine wise words to speak to you, which these
hobby-horses must not hear.
⌜*Benedick and Leonato exit.*⌝
PRINCE   For my life, to break with him about Beatrice!
CLAUDIO   'Tis even so. Hero and Margaret have by this   70
played their parts with Beatrice, and then the two
bears will not bite one another when they meet.

Enter John the Bastard.

DON JOHN   My lord and brother, God save you.
PRINCE   Good e'en, brother.
DON JOHN   If your leisure served, I would speak with   75
you.
PRINCE   In private?

80. **matter:** i.e., subject matter

86–87. **discover:** reveal

89. **hereafter:** later; **aim better at me:** judge me more highly or more accurately; **by that:** i.e., in the light of that which

90. **For:** i.e., as for

90–91. **holds you well:** i.e., thinks well of you

91. **dearness of heart:** i.e., affection; **holp:** i.e., helped; **effect:** bring about

95–96. **circumstances shortened:** i.e., to cut out the details

97. **a-talking of:** i.e., in our talking; **disloyal:** unfaithful, unchaste

102. **paint out:** i.e., depict, describe

105. **till . . . warrant:** i.e., until you have conclusive proof

112. **that you see:** i.e., that which you will see

113. **that you know:** i.e., that which you know

DON JOHN   If it please you. Yet Count Claudio may
hear, for what I would speak of concerns him.

PRINCE   What's the matter?   80

DON JOHN, ⌈*to Claudio*⌉   Means your Lordship to be
married tomorrow?

PRINCE   You know he does.

DON JOHN   I know not that, when he knows what I
know.   85

CLAUDIO   If there be any impediment, I pray you discover it.

DON JOHN   You may think I love you not. Let that
appear hereafter, and aim better at me by that I
now will manifest. For my brother, I think he holds   90
you well, and in dearness of heart hath holp to effect
your ensuing marriage—surely suit ill spent and
labor ill bestowed.

PRINCE   Why, what's the matter?

DON JOHN   I came hither to tell you; and, circum-   95
stances shortened, for she has been too long
a-talking of, the lady is disloyal.

CLAUDIO   Who, Hero?

DON JOHN   Even she: Leonato's Hero, your Hero, every
man's Hero.   100

CLAUDIO   Disloyal?

DON JOHN   The word is too good to paint out her
wickedness. I could say she were worse. Think you
of a worse title, and I will fit her to it. Wonder not
till further warrant. Go but with me tonight, you   105
shall see her chamber window entered, even the
night before her wedding day. If you love her then,
tomorrow wed her. But it would better fit your
honor to change your mind.

CLAUDIO, ⌈*to Prince*⌉   May this be so?   110

PRINCE   I will not think it.

DON JOHN   If you dare not trust that you see, confess
not that you know. If you will follow me, I will

119. **as:** i.e., since; or, in the same way that
122. **coldly:** coolly, calmly
123. **issue:** result (of what you see); **show:** reveal
125. **mischief:** evil, wickedness
126. **plague:** i.e., calamity
127. **the sequel:** that which follows

3.3 That night, Messina's master constable, Dogberry, and his assistant, Verges, set the night watch, telling the watchmen to pay particular attention to any activity around Leonato's house. Borachio enters, telling his companion, Conrade, about the charade that made Claudio and Don Pedro think that Hero had just allowed him to enter her chamber. Borachio and Conrade are arrested by the watch.

0 SD. **compartner:** copartner, associate; **Watch:** watchmen (citizens chosen to act as a night patrol)
2. **it were pity but they:** i.e., it would be regrettable if they did not
3. **salvation:** a mistake for "damnation"
5. **allegiance:** Dogberry seems to mean "lack of allegiance."
7. **charge:** i.e., orders
9. **most desartless:** i.e., least deserving (his mistake for "most deserving")
10. **constable:** perhaps, chief watchman (Dogberry himself is identified as "master constable"—officer of the peace—at line 17 and as *"the Constable"* in the opening stage direction of 3.5.)

show you enough, and when you have seen more
and heard more, proceed accordingly.   115
CLAUDIO If I see anything tonight why I should not
marry her, tomorrow in the congregation, where I
should wed, there will I shame her.
PRINCE And as I wooed for thee to obtain her, I will
join with thee to disgrace her.   120
DON JOHN I will disparage her no farther till you are
my witnesses. Bear it coldly but till midnight, and
let the issue show itself.
PRINCE O day untowardly turned!
CLAUDIO O mischief strangely thwarting!   125
DON JOHN O plague right well prevented! So will you
say when you have seen the sequel.
                                            ⌐*They exit.*⌐

⌐Scene 3⌐
Enter Dogberry and his compartner ⌐*Verges*⌐
with the Watch.

DOGBERRY Are you good men and true?
VERGES Yea, or else it were pity but they should suffer
salvation, body and soul.
DOGBERRY Nay, that were a punishment too good for
them if they should have any allegiance in them,   5
being chosen for the Prince's watch.
VERGES Well, give them their charge, neighbor Dogberry.
DOGBERRY First, who think you the most desartless
man to be constable?   10
FIRST WATCHMAN Hugh Oatcake, sir, or George Seacoal, for they can write and read.
DOGBERRY Come hither, neighbor Seacoal. ⌐*Seacoal
steps forward.*⌐ God hath blessed you with a good

15. **well-favored:** i.e., handsome

19. **favor:** appearance

22. **vanity:** perhaps, foolishness or worthlessness; or, perhaps, self-conceit; or, perhaps, a mistake for "talent"

23. **senseless:** a mistake for, perhaps, "sensible"

25. **comprehend:** a mistake for "apprehend," arrest; **vagrom:** i.e., vagrant, vagabond

26. **bid . . . stand:** i.e., order . . . to come to a halt

28. **take no note of:** i.e., pay no attention to

32. **none:** i.e., not one

36. **tolerable:** a mistake for "intolerable"

38. **belongs to:** i.e., is appropriate for

41. **bills:** long-handled pointed weapons carried by watchmen

50. **true:** honest; **for:** i.e., as for

A watchman.
From Thomas Dekker, *The belman of London* . . . (1616).

name. To be a well-favored man is the gift of   15
fortune, but to write and read comes by nature.
⌈SEACOAL⌉ Both which, master constable—
DOGBERRY You have. I knew it would be your answer.
Well, for your favor, sir, why, give God thanks, and
make no boast of it, and for your writing and   20
reading, let that appear when there is no need of
such vanity. You are thought here to be the most
senseless and fit man for the constable of the watch;
therefore bear you the lantern. This is your charge:
you shall comprehend all vagrom men; you are to   25
bid any man stand, in the Prince's name.
⌈SEACOAL⌉ How if he will not stand?
DOGBERRY Why, then, take no note of him, but let him
go, and presently call the rest of the watch together
and thank God you are rid of a knave.   30
VERGES If he will not stand when he is bidden, he is
none of the Prince's subjects.
DOGBERRY True, and they are to meddle with none but
the Prince's subjects.—You shall also make no
noise in the streets; for, for the watch to babble and   35
to talk is most tolerable and not to be endured.
⌈SECOND⌉ WATCHMAN We will rather sleep than talk.
We know what belongs to a watch.
DOGBERRY Why, you speak like an ancient and most
quiet watchman, for I cannot see how sleeping   40
should offend; only have a care that your bills be not
stolen. Well, you are to call at all the alehouses and
bid those that are drunk get them to bed.
⌈SEACOAL⌉ How if they will not?
DOGBERRY Why then, let them alone till they are sober.   45
If they make you not then the better answer, you
may say they are not the men you took them for.
⌈SEACOAL⌉ Well, sir.
DOGBERRY If you meet a thief, you may suspect him, by
virtue of your office, to be no true man, and for such   50

51. **meddle or make with:** have to do with (a proverbial expression)

52. **the more is:** i.e., the better it is

54. **lay hands on:** i.e., seize

56. **they . . . defiled:** proverbial

62. **by my will:** i.e., willingly

65. **still:** i.e., quiet

74. **present:** represent

75. **stay:** stop

76. **by 'r Lady:** an oath "by our Lady" (i.e., the Virgin Mary)

83. **An:** if

84. **there be . . . chances:** i.e., anything important happens

85. **Keep . . . counsels:** i.e., keep each other's secrets

Playing a tabor and pipe. (2.3.15)
From William Kemp,
Kempes nine daies wonder (1600; 1884 facs.).

kind of men, the less you meddle or make with
them, why, the more is for your honesty.
⌜SEACOAL⌝ If we know him to be a thief, shall we not
lay hands on him?
DOGBERRY Truly, by your office you may, but I think   55
they that touch pitch will be defiled. The most
peaceable way for you, if you do take a thief, is to
let him show himself what he is and steal out of
your company.
VERGES You have been always called a merciful man,   60
partner.
DOGBERRY Truly, I would not hang a dog by my will,
much more a man who hath any honesty in him.
VERGES, ⌜to the Watch⌝ If you hear a child cry in the
night, you must call to the nurse and bid her still it.   65
⌜SECOND⌝ WATCHMAN How if the nurse be asleep and
will not hear us?
DOGBERRY Why, then depart in peace, and let the
child wake her with crying, for the ewe that will
not hear her lamb when it baas will never answer a   70
calf when he bleats.
VERGES 'Tis very true.
DOGBERRY This is the end of the charge. You, constable, are to present the Prince's own person. If you
meet the Prince in the night, you may stay him.   75
VERGES Nay, by 'r Lady, that I think he cannot.
DOGBERRY Five shillings to one on 't, with any man that
knows the statutes, he may stay him—marry, not
without the Prince be willing, for indeed the watch
ought to offend no man, and it is an offense to stay a   80
man against his will.
VERGES By 'r Lady, I think it be so.
DOGBERRY Ha, ah ha!—Well, masters, goodnight. An
there be any matter of weight chances, call up me.
Keep your fellows' counsels and your own, and   85
goodnight.—Come, neighbor.
                    ⌜*Dogberry and Verges begin to exit.*⌝

92. **coil:** fuss, turmoil
93. **vigitant:** a mistake for "vigilant"
98. **Mass:** an oath "by the Mass"; **my elbow itched:** a proverbial warning against bad company
99. **scab:** (1) crust over a wound; (2) scoundrel
100. **answer:** return thrust (a fencing term)
102–3. **penthouse:** canopy; or, overhanging eaves
105. **treason:** treachery
105–6. **Yet stand close:** i.e., remain hidden
108. **ducats:** gold coins
110. **dear:** expensive, costly
112. **villainy:** perhaps, person who instigates wickedness
114. **make what price they will:** i.e., charge what they wish
115. **wonder:** i.e., am amazed
116. **unconfirmed:** ignorant, uninformed
117–18. **the fashion . . . man:** See longer note, page 202. **fashion:** style or cut **doublet:** short, close-fitting jacket

⌜SEACOAL⌝ Well, masters, we hear our charge. Let us go
sit here upon the church bench till two, and then all
to bed.

DOGBERRY One word more, honest neighbors. I pray   90
you watch about Signior Leonato's door, for the
wedding being there tomorrow, there is a great coil
tonight. Adieu, be vigitant, I beseech you.

⌜*Dogberry and Verges*⌝ *exit.*

Enter Borachio and Conrade.

BORACHIO What, Conrade!

⌜SEACOAL, *aside*⌝ Peace, stir not.   95

BORACHIO Conrade, I say!

CONRADE Here, man, I am at thy elbow.

BORACHIO Mass, and my elbow itched, I thought there
would a scab follow.

CONRADE I will owe thee an answer for that. And now   100
forward with thy tale.

BORACHIO Stand thee close, then, under this penthouse, for it drizzles rain, and I will, like a true
drunkard, utter all to thee.

⌜SEACOAL, *aside*⌝ Some treason, masters. Yet stand   105
close.

BORACHIO Therefore know, I have earned of ⌜Don⌝
John a thousand ducats.

CONRADE Is it possible that any villainy should be so
dear?   110

BORACHIO Thou shouldst rather ask if it were possible
any villainy should be so rich. For when rich
villains have need of poor ones, poor ones may
make what price they will.

CONRADE I wonder at it.   115

BORACHIO That shows thou art unconfirmed. Thou
knowest that the fashion of a doublet, or a hat, or a
cloak, is nothing to a man.

121. **the fashion:** perhaps, that which is fashionable; what people are currently wearing

123-24. **this fashion:** i.e., fashion, that which is fashionable

126-27. **up and down:** i.e., here and there

132. **hot bloods:** i.e., hot-blooded young men

133. **fashioning:** dressing; **Pharaoh:** in the Bible, the king of Egypt from whom the Israelites fled

134. **reechy:** smoky, dirty

134-35. **Bel's priests:** i.e., the priests of Baal in the Apocrypha

135. **old . . . window:** i.e., stained-glass church window

136. **Hercules:** See notes to 2.1.250 and 251, and page 146. The reference to Hercules as shaven has not been satisfactorily explained.

137. **codpiece:** a showy attachment to the front of a man's breeches; **massy:** massive, huge

139-40. **fashion . . . man:** i.e., changes in fashion cause clothes to be discarded more than do wear and tear

146. **by the name of Hero:** i.e., calling her "Hero"; **leans me:** i.e., leans

150. **possessed:** given information

151. **amiable:** amorous

CONRADE   Yes, it is apparel.

BORACHIO   I mean the fashion.   120

CONRADE   Yes, the fashion is the fashion.

BORACHIO   Tush, I may as well say the fool's the fool.
But seest thou not what a deformed thief this
fashion is?

⌐FIRST⌐ WATCHMAN, ⌐*aside*⌐ I know that Deformed. He   125
has been a vile thief this seven year. He goes up and
down like a gentleman. I remember his name.

BORACHIO   Didst thou not hear somebody?

CONRADE   No, 'twas the vane on the house.

BORACHIO   Seest thou not, I say, what a deformed thief   130
this fashion is, how giddily he turns about all the
hot bloods between fourteen and five-and-thirty,
sometimes fashioning them like Pharaoh's soldiers
in the reechy painting, sometimes like god Bel's
priests in the old church window, sometimes like   135
the shaven Hercules in the smirched worm-eaten
tapestry, where his codpiece seems as massy as his
club?

CONRADE   All this I see, and I see that the fashion wears
out more apparel than the man. But art not thou   140
thyself giddy with the fashion too, that thou hast
shifted out of thy tale into telling me of the
fashion?

BORACHIO   Not so, neither. But know that I have tonight wooed Margaret, the Lady Hero's gentle-   145
woman, by the name of Hero. She leans me out at
her mistress' chamber window, bids me a thousand
times goodnight. I tell this tale vilely. I should first
tell thee how the Prince, Claudio, and my master,
planted and placed and possessed by my master   150
Don John, saw afar off in the orchard this amiable
encounter.

CONRADE   And thought they Margaret was Hero?

BORACHIO   Two of them did, the Prince and Claudio,

156. **possessed:** influenced (but with a sense of demonic possession)

160–61. **as he was appointed:** i.e., as had been arranged (literally, as he had an appointment to do)

163. **o'ernight:** the preceding evening

168. **recovered:** a mistake for "discovered"

169. **lechery:** perhaps he means "villainy" or, perhaps, "treachery"

172. **lock:** a long lock of hair

172 SD. **Enter Dogberry:** See longer note, page 202.

174. **made bring:** i.e., forced to bring

177. **obey:** perhaps, order (or perhaps he is trying to say, "Obey us and go with us")

178. **like:** likely

179. **commodity:** parcel of goods; **being taken up:** To "take up a commodity" was to obtain goods on credit and then sell them for cash. **bills:** (1) watchmen's weapons; (2) "bills of parcels" or itemized invoices

180. **in question:** in dispute; or, in a doubtful state

but the devil my master knew she was Margaret;   155
and partly by his oaths, which first possessed them,
partly by the dark night, which did deceive them,
but chiefly by my villainy, which did confirm any
slander that Don John had made, away went Claudio
enraged, swore he would meet her as he was   160
appointed next morning at the temple, and there,
before the whole congregation, shame her with
what he saw o'ernight and send her home again
without a husband.

FIRST WATCHMAN   We charge you in the Prince's name,   165
stand!

⌜SEACOAL⌝   Call up the right Master Constable. ⌜*Second
Watchman exits.*⌝ We have here recovered the most
dangerous piece of lechery that ever was known in
the commonwealth.   170

FIRST WATCHMAN   And one Deformed is one of them. I
know him; he wears a lock.

⌜*Enter Dogberry, Verges, and Second Watchman.*⌝

⌜DOGBERRY⌝   Masters, masters—

⌜FIRST⌝ WATCHMAN, ⌜*to Borachio*⌝   You'll be made bring
Deformed forth, I warrant you.   175

⌜DOGBERRY, *to Borachio and Conrade*⌝   Masters, never
speak, we charge you, let us obey you to go with us.

BORACHIO, ⌜*to Conrade*⌝   We are like to prove a goodly
commodity, being taken up of these men's bills.

CONRADE   A commodity in question, I warrant you.—   180
Come, we'll obey you.

They exit.

3.4 Early the next morning, Hero prepares for the wedding. Beatrice enters, suffering, she says, from a bad cold, but Hero and Margaret tease her about being in love with Benedick.

------

2. **desire:** i.e., tell
5. **Well:** i.e., very well
6. **Troth:** a mild oath; **rebato:** a tall, ornamental, stiff collar
8. **pray thee:** a phrase of apology
9. **'s:** i.e., it is
13. **tire:** attire, headdress; **within:** perhaps, in the next room
14. **hair:** i.e., hairpiece attached to the headdress; **a thought:** i.e., a bit
17. **that exceeds:** i.e., that's wonderful
18. **nightgown:** dressing gown
18–19. **in respect of:** i.e., compared to
19. **cloth o' gold:** fabric woven in part from gold thread; **cuts:** slashes in the outer fabric that show off the rich lining
19–20. **laced with silver:** i.e., trimmed with silver lace
20. **down sleeves:** tight-fitting long sleeves; **side sleeves:** long ornamental sleeves hanging from the shoulder
21. **underborne:** trimmed underneath; **tinsel:** rich fabric interwoven with silver or gold
22. **quaint:** elaborate, elegant
23. **on 't:** i.e., of it
25. **heavy:** sad, somber
30. **in a beggar:** i.e., even in a beggar

(continued)

⌜Scene 4⌝

Enter Hero, and Margaret, and Ursula.

HERO Good Ursula, wake my cousin Beatrice and
desire her to rise.

URSULA I will, lady.

HERO And bid her come hither.

URSULA Well.   ⌜*Ursula exits.*⌝ 5

MARGARET Troth, I think your other rebato were
better.

HERO No, pray thee, good Meg, I'll wear this.

MARGARET By my troth, 's not so good, and I warrant
your cousin will say so.   10

HERO My cousin's a fool, and thou art another. I'll
wear none but this.

MARGARET I like the new tire within excellently, if the
hair were a thought browner; and your gown's a
most rare fashion, i' faith. I saw the Duchess of   15
Milan's gown that they praise so.

HERO O, that exceeds, they say.

MARGARET By my troth, 's but a nightgown ⌜in⌝ respect
of yours—cloth o' gold, and cuts, and laced with
silver, set with pearls, down sleeves, side sleeves,   20
and skirts round underborne with a bluish tinsel.
But for a fine, quaint, graceful, and excellent fashion, yours is worth ten on 't.

HERO God give me joy to wear it, for my heart is
exceeding heavy.   25

MARGARET 'Twill be heavier soon by the weight of a
man.

HERO Fie upon thee! Art not ashamed?

MARGARET Of what, lady? Of speaking honorably? Is
not marriage honorable in a beggar? Is not your   30
lord honorable without marriage? I think you
would have me say "Saving your reverence, a husband." An bad thinking do not wrest true speaking,

32. **Saving your reverence:** a request to be excused for using an indecent word

33. **An:** if; **do not wrest:** i.e., does not distort or twist the meaning of

36. **light:** licentious; or, frivolous

37. **heavy:** serious (with the obvious puns on both words); **else:** i.e., if you doubt me

41. **in the sick tune:** i.e., as if you were sick

43. **Clap 's into:** i.e., let's clap (swing) into; **Light o' love:** the name of a popular song

44. **burden:** refrain; or bass accompaniment (The standard meaning of **burden** picks up the word **heavier** in line 26 and continues the puns on **light** and **heavy.**)

45. **light o' love with your heels:** a double accusation of wantonness (**light** meaning licentious and "light-heeled" meaning "unchaste")

47. **barns:** contains a pun on "bairns" or children

48. **illegitimate:** inaccurate (with the obvious pun); **construction:** interpretation

48–49. **scorn that with my heels:** proverbial, meaning to reject something with contempt

52–53. **Heigh-ho . . . husband:** See note to 2.1.313.

54. **H:** The noun form of *ache* was pronounced like the letter *h*. The pun on *h* and *ache* was common.

55. **turned Turk:** i.e., renounced your old faith

55–56. **there's . . . star:** i.e., there's nothing one can trust (literally, one cannot use the North Star for navigation)

57. **trow:** i.e., I trow, I wonder

60. **they are:** i.e., they have

62. **I am stuffed:** i.e., my nose is stuffed up

(continued)

I'll offend nobody. Is there any harm in "the heavier
for a husband"? None, I think, an it be the right   35
husband and the right wife. Otherwise, 'tis light and
not heavy. Ask my lady Beatrice else. Here she
comes.

Enter Beatrice.

HERO   Good morrow, coz.
BEATRICE   Good morrow, sweet Hero.   40
HERO   Why, how now? Do you speak in the sick tune?
BEATRICE   I am out of all other tune, methinks.
MARGARET   Clap 's into "Light o' love." That goes
without a burden. Do you sing it, and I'll dance it.
BEATRICE   You light o' love with your heels! Then, if   45
your husband have stables enough, you'll see he
shall lack no barns.
MARGARET   O, illegitimate construction! I scorn that
with my heels.
BEATRICE   'Tis almost five o'clock, cousin. 'Tis time   50
you were ready. By my troth, I am exceeding ill.
Heigh-ho!
MARGARET   For a hawk, a horse, or a husband?
BEATRICE   For the letter that begins them all, *H*.
MARGARET   Well, an you be not turned Turk, there's no   55
more sailing by the star.
BEATRICE   What means the fool, trow?
MARGARET   Nothing, I; but God send everyone their
heart's desire.
HERO   These gloves the Count sent me, they are an   60
excellent perfume.
BEATRICE   I am stuffed, cousin. I cannot smell.
MARGARET   A maid, and stuffed! There's goodly catch-
ing of cold.
BEATRICE   O, God help me, God help me! How long   65
have you professed apprehension?

63. **stuffed:** perhaps, pregnant
66. **professed apprehension:** i.e., made wittiness your profession
67. **it:** i.e., **apprehension,** wit
68. **rarely:** excellently
71. **some of this:** i.e., some
71-72. **carduus benedictus:** i.e., the herb "blessed thistle," which was claimed to be "a salve for every sore" (Lines 71-76 pun on **carduus**—which means "thistle" and which sounds like the Latin *cordis,* "of the heart"—and on **benedictus,** which means "holy" and which contains Benedick's name.)
73. **qualm:** sudden illness
76. **moral:** hidden meaning
80. **list:** choose
84. **such another:** i.e., another who refused to love
86. **in despite of:** i.e., despite the opposition of
86-87. **eats . . . grudging:** perhaps, is content to be like other men
91. **false gallop:** literally, a canter (with a pun on **false** as "untrue, mistaken")

Blessed thistle *(Carduus benedictus).*
From John Gerard, *The herball . . .* (1597).

MARGARET Ever since you left it. Doth not my wit
become me rarely?
BEATRICE It is not seen enough; you should wear it in
your cap. By my troth, I am sick.   70
MARGARET Get you some of this distilled *carduus benedictus* and lay it to your heart. It is the only thing for
a qualm.
HERO There thou prick'st her with a thistle.
BEATRICE *Benedictus!* Why *benedictus?* You have some   75
moral in this *benedictus?*
MARGARET Moral? No, by my troth, I have no moral
meaning; I meant plain holy thistle. You may think
perchance that I think you are in love. Nay, by 'r
Lady, I am not such a fool to think what I list, nor I   80
list not to think what I can, nor indeed I cannot
think, if I would think my heart out of thinking, that
you are in love or that you will be in love or that you
can be in love. Yet Benedick was such another, and
now is he become a man. He swore he would never   85
marry, and yet now, in despite of his heart, he eats
his meat without grudging. And how you may be
converted I know not, but methinks you look with
your eyes as other women do.
BEATRICE What pace is this that thy tongue keeps?   90
MARGARET Not a false gallop.

Enter Ursula.

URSULA Madam, withdraw. The Prince, the Count,
Signior Benedick, Don John, and all the gallants of
the town are come to fetch you to church.
HERO Help to dress me, good coz, good Meg, good   95
Ursula.
                                             ⌜*They exit.*⌝

3.5 Dogberry and Verges try to tell Leonato about the arrest of Borachio and Conrade, but they are so unintelligible that Leonato impatiently dismisses them, telling them to examine the prisoners. He leaves for the wedding.

———

0 SD. **Headborough:** constable with more limited authority than Dogberry's

2. **confidence:** a mistake for "conference, conversation"

3. **decerns:** a mistake for "concerns"; **nearly:** closely

9. **Goodman:** a term of address for a man below the rank of gentleman

10. **blunt:** a mistake for "sharp"

12. **honest . . . brows:** proverbial

15. **odorous:** Proverbial: "Comparisons are odious." **Palabras:** The Spanish phrase *pocas palabras* means "few words."

19. **the poor duke's officers:** a mistake for "the duke's poor officers"

20. **tedious as a king:** The following lines indicate that Dogberry thinks **tedious** means "rich."

21. **of:** i.e., on

23. **an 'twere:** if it were

24. **exclamation on:** probably a mistake for "acclamations of" ("To exclaim on" meant "to accuse loudly, to blame.")

28. **fain:** gladly

29. **tonight:** last night

(continued)

⌐Scene 5⌐
Enter Leonato, and ⌐Dogberry,⌐ the Constable, and
⌐Verges,⌐ the Headborough.

LEONATO   What would you with me, honest neighbor?

DOGBERRY   Marry, sir, I would have some confidence
with you that decerns you nearly.

LEONATO   Brief, I pray you, for you see it is a busy time
with me.   5

DOGBERRY   Marry, this it is, sir.

VERGES   Yes, in truth, it is, sir.

LEONATO   What is it, my good friends?

DOGBERRY   Goodman Verges, sir, speaks a little off the
matter. An old man, sir, and his wits are not so blunt   10
as, God help, I would desire they were, but, in faith,
honest as the skin between his brows.

VERGES   Yes, I thank God I am as honest as any man
living that is an old man and no honester than I.

DOGBERRY   Comparisons are odorous. *Palabras,* neigh-   15
bor Verges.

LEONATO   Neighbors, you are tedious.

DOGBERRY   It pleases your Worship to say so, but we
are the poor duke's officers. But truly, for mine
own part, if I were as tedious as a king, I could find   20
in my heart to bestow it all of your Worship.

LEONATO   All thy tediousness on me, ah?

DOGBERRY   Yea, an 'twere a thousand pound more
than 'tis, for I hear as good exclamation on your
Worship as of any man in the city, and though I be   25
but a poor man, I am glad to hear it.

VERGES   And so am I.

LEONATO   I would fain know what you have to say.

VERGES   Marry, sir, our watch tonight, excepting your
Worship's presence, ha' ta'en a couple of as arrant   30
knaves as any in Messina.

DOGBERRY   A good old man, sir. He will be talking. As

29–30. **excepting . . . presence:** Dogberry probably intends the complimentary phrase "respecting [showing respect to] your presence." (His words mean, literally, "except for you, the men we have arrested are 'as arrant knaves as any in Messina.' ")

30. **ha' ta'en:** i.e., have taken, have arrested

31. **knaves:** villains

33. **age:** The proverb actually states: "When the ale is in, the wit is out." (The rest of this speech is a collection of proverbs that are more accurately reproduced than this one.)

36. **ride of a horse:** i.e., ride on one horse

40. **he comes too short of you:** i.e., he can't measure up to you

41. **Gifts:** i.e., my virtues are gifts

44. **comprehended:** a mistake for "apprehended"; **aspicious:** a mistake for "suspicious"

50. **suffigance:** a mistake for "sufficient"

52. **stay:** i.e., wait

54. **wait upon:** attend

55–56. **Francis Seacoal:** This may be the Sexton who appears in 4.2. The watchman in 3.2 was named George Seacoal.

57. **examination:** a mistake for "examine"

59. **spare for no wit:** i.e., not hold back on wisdom

60. **noncome:** perhaps a confusion of *non plus* ("a state of perplexity") with *non compos mentis* ("not of sound mind")

61–62. **excommunication:** a mistake for "examination"

they say, "When the age is in, the wit is out." God
help us, it is a world to see!—Well said, i' faith,
neighbor Verges.—Well, God's a good man. An two   35
men ride of a horse, one must ride behind. An
honest soul, i' faith, sir, by my troth he is, as ever
broke bread, but God is to be worshiped, all men
are not alike, alas, good neighbor.

LEONATO   Indeed, neighbor, he comes too short of you.   40

DOGBERRY   Gifts that God gives.

LEONATO   I must leave you.

DOGBERRY   One word, sir. Our watch, sir, have indeed
comprehended two aspicious persons, and we
would have them this morning examined before   45
your Worship.

LEONATO   Take their examination yourself and bring it
me. I am now in great haste, as it may appear unto
you.

DOGBERRY   It shall be suffigance.   50

LEONATO   Drink some wine ere you go. Fare you well.

⌜*Enter a Messenger.*⌝

MESSENGER   My lord, they stay for you to give your
daughter to her husband.

LEONATO   I'll wait upon them. I am ready.

He exits, ⌜*with the Messenger.*⌝

DOGBERRY   Go, good partner, go, get you to Francis   55
Seacoal. Bid him bring his pen and inkhorn to the
jail. We are now to examination these men.

VERGES   And we must do it wisely.

DOGBERRY   We will spare for no wit, I warrant you.
Here's that shall drive some of them to a noncome.   60
Only get the learned writer to set down our excom-
munication and meet me at the jail.

⌜*They exit.*⌝

MUCH ADO
ABOUT NOTHING

ACT 4

4.1 At the wedding, Claudio publicly denounces Hero as a lewd woman. He is supported in his story by Don Pedro and Don John. Hero faints and her accusers depart. The Friar believes in her innocence and proposes that Leonato announce that she has died. This news, the Friar thinks, will make Claudio remember his love for her. After the others depart, Benedick and Beatrice admit they love each other, and Benedick reluctantly agrees to challenge Claudio to a duel.

---

    12. **inward:** undisclosed
    13. **charge:** command
    21–22. **some . . . ha, he:** an echo of Lyly's Latin *Grammar*, where **interjections** are defined

A lute. (2.1.92, 2.3.61)
From Silvestro Pietrasanta,
Symbola heroica . . . (1682).

⌜ACT 4⌝

⌜Scene 1⌝

Enter Prince, ⌜John the⌝ Bastard, Leonato, Friar,
Claudio, Benedick, Hero, and Beatrice, ⌜with
Attendants.⌝

LEONATO Come, Friar Francis, be brief, only to the
plain form of marriage, and you shall recount their
particular duties afterwards.

FRIAR, ⌜*to Claudio*⌝ You come hither, my lord, to marry
this lady?   5

CLAUDIO No.

LEONATO To be married to her.—Friar, you come to
marry her.

FRIAR Lady, you come hither to be married to this
count?   10

HERO I do.

FRIAR If either of you know any inward impediment
why you should not be conjoined, I charge you on
your souls to utter it.

CLAUDIO Know you any, Hero?   15

HERO None, my lord.

FRIAR Know you any, count?

LEONATO I dare make his answer, none.

CLAUDIO O, what men dare do! What men may do!
What men daily do, not knowing what they do!   20

BENEDICK How now, interjections? Why, then, some
be of laughing, as ah, ha, he!

123

23. **Stand thee by:** i.e., stand aside
30. **learn:** i.e., teach
33. **sign:** show or pretense
35. **authority:** power to inspire belief; **show:** outward appearance
36. **withal:** i.e., with
37. **modest evidence:** i.e., evidence of modesty
38. **witness:** i.e., act as a witness to
41. **luxurious:** lascivious, lecherous
45. **approvèd:** proved, convicted
46. **proof:** perhaps, experience; or, perhaps, trial or test of her
49. **known:** had sexual relations with
50. **embrace me as a husband:** Although the church forbade intercourse before the ritual celebration of marriage, the law allowed intercourse for formally betrothed couples.

CLAUDIO
  Stand thee by, friar.—Father, by your leave,
  Will you with free and unconstrainèd soul
  Give me this maid, your daughter?   25
LEONATO
  As freely, son, as God did give her me.
CLAUDIO
  And what have I to give you back whose worth
  May counterpoise this rich and precious gift?
PRINCE
  Nothing, unless you render her again.
CLAUDIO
  Sweet prince, you learn me noble thankfulness.—   30
  There, Leonato, take her back again.
  Give not this rotten orange to your friend.
  She's but the sign and semblance of her honor.
  Behold how like a maid she blushes here!
  O, what authority and show of truth   35
  Can cunning sin cover itself withal!
  Comes not that blood as modest evidence
  To witness simple virtue? Would you not swear,
  All you that see her, that she were a maid,
  By these exterior shows? But she is none.   40
  She knows the heat of a luxurious bed.
  Her blush is guiltiness, not modesty.
LEONATO
  What do you mean, my lord?
CLAUDIO   Not to be married,
  Not to knit my soul to an approvèd wanton.   45
LEONATO
  Dear my lord, if you in your own proof
  Have vanquished the resistance of her youth,
  And made defeat of her virginity—
CLAUDIO
  I know what you would say: if I have known her,
  You will say she did embrace me as a husband,   50

51. **forehand sin:** i.e., the sinfulness of the act committed in anticipation (of the marriage)

53. **too large:** improper, gross

55. **comely:** proper, decorous

57. **Out on thee:** i.e., curses on you; **seeming:** semblance, mere appearance

58. **Dian:** i.e., Diana, goddess of chastity and of the moon (here equated with the moon "in her [i.e., its] orb"); **orb:** sphere (In Ptolemaic astronomy, the moon, like the sun and the planets, moved around the earth in its own crystalline sphere.)

59. **be blown:** i.e., has burst into flower

60. **blood:** sensual appetites

61. **Venus:** goddess of love, often depicted as promiscuous and highly sensual

63. **wide:** i.e., wide of the mark, wildly

68. **common stale:** lowest-class prostitute

72. **True:** an echo of Don John's word at line 70

77. **but move:** only pose

"Dian in her orb." (4.1.58)
From Vincenzo Cartari,
Le vere e noue Imagini . . . (1615).

And so extenuate the forehand sin.
No, Leonato,
I never tempted her with word too large,
But, as a brother to his sister, showed
Bashful sincerity and comely love.   55
HERO
And seemed I ever otherwise to you?
CLAUDIO
Out on thee, seeming! I will write against it.
You seem to me as Dian in her orb,
As chaste as is the bud ere it be blown.
But you are more intemperate in your blood   60
Than Venus, or those pampered animals
That rage in savage sensuality.
HERO
Is my lord well that he doth speak so wide?
LEONATO
Sweet prince, why speak not you?
PRINCE   What should I   65
    speak?
I stand dishonored that have gone about
To link my dear friend to a common stale.
LEONATO
Are these things spoken, or do I but dream?
DON JOHN
Sir, they are spoken, and these things are true.   70
BENEDICK   This looks not like a nuptial.
HERO   True! O God!
CLAUDIO   Leonato, stand I here?
Is this the Prince? Is this the Prince's brother?
Is this face Hero's? Are our eyes our own?   75
LEONATO
All this is so, but what of this, my lord?
CLAUDIO
Let me but move one question to your daughter,

78. **kindly:** lawful
80. **charge thee:** order you to
86. **Marry:** an oath "by the Virgin Mary"
87. **Hero itself can blot out Hero's virtue:** See longer note, page 203.
92. **Why . . . maiden:** Since she does not answer his question by naming the man, she fails his test: "if you are a maid, answer. . . ."
94. **grievèd:** aggrieved; grief-stricken
97. **liberal:** plainspoken
104. **much misgovernment:** great immorality

And by that fatherly and kindly power
That you have in her, bid her answer truly.

LEONATO
I charge thee do so, as thou art my child.   80

HERO
O, God defend me, how am I beset!—
What kind of catechizing call you this?

CLAUDIO
To make you answer truly to your name.

HERO
Is it not Hero? Who can blot that name
With any just reproach?   85

CLAUDIO   Marry, that can Hero!
Hero itself can blot out Hero's virtue.
What man was he talked with you yesternight
Out at your window betwixt twelve and one?
Now, if you are a maid, answer to this.   90

HERO
I talked with no man at that hour, my lord.

PRINCE
Why, then, are you no maiden.—Leonato,
I am sorry you must hear. Upon mine honor,
Myself, my brother, and this grievèd count
Did see her, hear her, at that hour last night   95
Talk with a ruffian at her chamber window,
Who hath indeed, most like a liberal villain,
Confessed the vile encounters they have had
A thousand times in secret.

DON JOHN
Fie, fie, they are not to be named, my lord,   100
Not to be spoke of!
There is not chastity enough in language,
Without offense, to utter them.—Thus, pretty lady,
I am sorry for thy much misgovernment.

CLAUDIO
O Hero, what a Hero hadst thou been   105

106. **outward graces:** external beauties
110. **For:** i.e., because of
111. **conjecture:** suspicion
112. **thoughts of harm:** i.e., harmful thoughts; or, perhaps, thoughts about harm
113. **gracious:** attractive (to me)
115. **wherefore:** why
117. **spirits:** vital powers
122. **cover:** screen, concealment, cloak
130. **blood:** i.e., blushes

If half thy outward graces had been placed
About thy thoughts and counsels of thy heart!
But fare thee well, most foul, most fair. Farewell,
Thou pure impiety and impious purity.
For thee I'll lock up all the gates of love   110
And on my eyelids shall conjecture hang,
To turn all beauty into thoughts of harm,
And never shall it more be gracious.

LEONATO
Hath no man's dagger here a point for me?
                                        ⌜*Hero falls.*⌝
BEATRICE
Why, how now, cousin, wherefore sink you down?   115
DON JOHN
Come, let us go. These things, come thus to light,
Smother her spirits up.
                    ⌜*Claudio, Prince, and Don John exit.*⌝
BENEDICK
How doth the lady?
BEATRICE   Dead, I think.—Help, uncle!—
Hero, why Hero! Uncle! Signior Benedick! Friar!   120
LEONATO
O Fate, take not away thy heavy hand!
Death is the fairest cover for her shame
That may be wished for.
BEATRICE   How now, cousin Hero?   ⌜*Hero stirs.*⌝
FRIAR, ⌜*to Hero*⌝   Have comfort, lady.   125
LEONATO, ⌜*to Hero*⌝
Dost thou look up?
FRIAR   Yea, wherefore should she not?
LEONATO
Wherefore? Why, doth not every earthly thing
Cry shame upon her? Could she here deny
The story that is printed in her blood?—   130
Do not live, Hero, do not ope thine eyes,
For, did I think thou wouldst not quickly die,

134. **on the rearward of reproaches:** i.e., after reproaching you; or, after this public scandal

136. **Chid:** i.e., chided, found fault, uttered words of rebuke; **frame:** plan

137. **much:** i.e., many

140. **issue:** i.e., infant

141. **mired:** soiled

145. **proud on:** i.e., proud of

147. **Valuing of:** i.e., because I cared so much for

148. **that the:** i.e., so that the

150–51. **season give / To:** (1) preserve from decay (literally, embalm); (2) restore to soundness (literally, add flavor or relish to)

153. **wonder:** amazement

155. **is belied:** i.e., has been lied about

160. **before:** i.e., already

Thought I thy spirits were stronger than thy shames,
Myself would, on the rearward of reproaches,
Strike at thy life. Grieved I I had but one?   135
Chid I for that at frugal Nature's frame?
O, one too much by thee! Why had I one?
Why ever wast thou lovely in my eyes?
Why had I not with charitable hand
Took up a beggar's issue at my gates,   140
Who, smirchèd thus, and mired with infamy,
I might have said "No part of it is mine;
This shame derives itself from unknown loins"?
But mine, and mine I loved, and mine I praised,
And mine that I was proud on, mine so much   145
That I myself was to myself not mine,
Valuing of her—why she, O she, is fall'n
Into a pit of ink, that the wide sea
Hath drops too few to wash her clean again,
And salt too little which may season give   150
To her foul tainted flesh!
BENEDICK   Sir, sir, be patient.
For my part, I am so attired in wonder
I know not what to say.
BEATRICE
O, on my soul, my cousin is belied!   155
BENEDICK
Lady, were you her bedfellow last night?
BEATRICE
No, truly not, although until last night
I have this twelvemonth been her bedfellow.
LEONATO
Confirmed, confirmed! O, that is stronger made
Which was before barred up with ribs of iron!   160
Would the two princes lie and Claudio lie,
Who loved her so that, speaking of her foulness,
Washed it with tears? Hence from her. Let her die!
FRIAR   Hear me a little,

166. **given way . . . fortune:** i.e., accepted this course of events

167. **noting of:** paying attention to; **marked:** noticed

168, 169. **blushing apparitions, shames:** The Friar describes Hero's alternately red and white face as if it were being visited by supernatural beings.

169. **start into:** i.e., appear suddenly in

172. **burn the errors:** an image in which the **errors** are heretics to be burned at the stake

174. **reading:** perhaps, reading of Hero's face

175. **experimental seal:** i.e., the seal of experience; **warrant:** guarantee (the truth of)

176. **tenor of my book:** i.e., what I find in my reading (The reference here is either to the books he has read or to Hero's face, which he reads as if it were a book.)

177. **reverence:** perhaps, age, position as a venerable person; **calling:** profession as priest; **divinity:** knowledge of theology

181. **grace:** goodness, virtue

188. **of:** i.e., about

189. **warrant:** sanction, allow

191. **Prove you:** i.e., if you prove

192. **unmeet:** unfitting, improper

193. **Maintained . . . words:** i.e., talked

194. **Refuse:** reject, abandon

195. **misprision:** misunderstanding, error

196. **have the very bent of honor:** i.e., are totally disposed to be honorable

For I have only ⌈silent been⌉ so long,   165
And given way unto this course of fortune,
By noting of the lady. I have marked
A thousand blushing apparitions
To start into her face, a thousand innocent shames
In angel whiteness beat away those blushes,   170
And in her eye there hath appeared a fire
To burn the errors that these princes hold
Against her maiden truth. Call me a fool,
Trust not my reading nor my observations,
Which with experimental seal doth warrant   175
The tenor of my book; trust not my age,
My reverence, calling, nor divinity,
If this sweet lady lie not guiltless here
Under some biting error.

LEONATO   Friar, it cannot be.   180
Thou seest that all the grace that she hath left
Is that she will not add to her damnation
A sin of perjury. She not denies it.
Why seek'st thou then to cover with excuse
That which appears in proper nakedness?   185

FRIAR
Lady, what man is he you are accused of?

HERO
They know that do accuse me. I know none.
If I know more of any man alive
Than that which maiden modesty doth warrant,
Let all my sins lack mercy!—O my father,   190
Prove you that any man with me conversed
At hours unmeet, or that I yesternight
Maintained the change of words with any creature,
Refuse me, hate me, torture me to death!

FRIAR
There is some strange misprision in the princes.   195

BENEDICK
Two of them have the very bent of honor,

197. **wisdoms:** understanding, good judgment
198. **practice:** machination, plotting
199. **spirits:** vital powers; **frame of:** i.e., framing, contriving
200. **but:** merely
204. **invention:** inventiveness, ability to plot or scheme
206. **reft:** i.e., bereft, deprived
207. **kind:** manner
208. **policy:** cunning
210. **quit me of:** repay, settle the score with; **throughly:** i.e., thoroughly
215. **publish:** proclaim
216. **mourning ostentation:** display or show of mourning
217. **monument:** sepulcher, burial vault
220. **become of:** i.e., come from
221. **carried:** managed
223. **dream . . . on:** conceive . . . of, think . . . of
224. **on this travail:** i.e., from this effort (with a pun on **travail** as childbirth)
225. **maintained:** declared to be true
228. **Of:** i.e., by
229. **prize:** esteem, value; **the worth:** i.e., its true value

And if their wisdoms be misled in this,
The practice of it lives in John the Bastard,
Whose spirits toil in frame of villainies.
LEONATO
I know not. If they speak but truth of her,   200
These hands shall tear her. If they wrong her honor,
The proudest of them shall well hear of it.
Time hath not yet so dried this blood of mine,
Nor age so eat up my invention,
Nor fortune made such havoc of my means,   205
Nor my bad life reft me so much of friends,
But they shall find, awaked in such a kind,
Both strength of limb and policy of mind,
Ability in means and choice of friends,
To quit me of them throughly.   210
FRIAR   Pause awhile,
And let my counsel sway you in this case.
Your daughter here the princes left for dead.
Let her awhile be secretly kept in,
And publish it that she is dead indeed.   215
Maintain a mourning ostentation,
And on your family's old monument
Hang mournful epitaphs and do all rites
That appertain unto a burial.
LEONATO
What shall become of this? What will this do?   220
FRIAR
Marry, this well carried shall on her behalf
Change slander to remorse. That is some good.
But not for that dream I on this strange course,
But on this travail look for greater birth.
She, dying, as it must be so maintained,   225
Upon the instant that she was accused,
Shall be lamented, pitied, and excused
Of every hearer. For it so falls out
That what we have we prize not to the worth

231. **rack the value:** i.e., strain its worth to the limit

232. **possession:** i.e., possessing it

233. **fare:** happen

236. **study of imagination:** imaginative reveries

237. **every . . . life:** i.e., all that gives her life **organ:** a means of action or operation

238. **habit:** clothing

240. **prospect:** range of vision

242. **interest in:** a claim upon, a share in; **liver:** thought to be the seat of the passions

245. **doubt not but:** i.e., do not doubt that; **success:** i.e., that which follows

246. **event:** outcome

247. **lay . . . likelihood:** i.e., project as its probable outcome

248. **if all . . . false:** i.e., if we miss the mark in everything but **this** (i.e., the **supposition of the lady's death**)

251. **it sort not:** i.e., it does not turn out

253. **reclusive:** cloistered

254. **injuries:** insults

256. **inwardness:** close friendship

261. **Being that:** i.e., since; **flow in:** perhaps, am flooded with, or am afloat in

263. **Presently:** at once

Whiles we enjoy it, but being lacked and lost,   230
Why then we rack the value, then we find
The virtue that possession would not show us
Whiles it was ours. So will it fare with Claudio.
When he shall hear she died upon his words,
Th' idea of her life shall sweetly creep   235
Into his study of imagination,
And every lovely organ of her life
Shall come appareled in more precious habit,
More moving, delicate, and full of life,
Into the eye and prospect of his soul,   240
Than when she lived indeed. Then shall he mourn,
If ever love had interest in his liver,
And wish he had not so accused her,
No, though he thought his accusation true.
Let this be so, and doubt not but success   245
Will fashion the event in better shape
Than I can lay it down in likelihood.
But if all aim but this be leveled false,
The supposition of the lady's death
Will quench the wonder of her infamy.   250
And if it sort not well, you may conceal her,
As best befits her wounded reputation,
In some reclusive and religious life,
Out of all eyes, tongues, minds, and injuries.
BENEDICK
    Signior Leonato, let the Friar advise you.   255
    And though you know my inwardness and love
    Is very much unto the Prince and Claudio,
    Yet, by mine honor, I will deal in this
    As secretly and justly as your soul
    Should with your body.   260
LEONATO   Being that I flow in grief,
    The smallest twine may lead me.
FRIAR
    'Tis well consented. Presently away,

264. **to strange sores:** i.e., to heal unusual wounds; **strangely:** in extraordinary ways

264–65. **they strain the cure:** i.e., people use extraordinary remedies

267. **prolonged:** postponed

278. **even:** direct, straightforward

279. **May:** i.e., can

280. **office:** function, job

288. **By my sword:** a mild oath

289–93. **swear and eat it . . . devised to it:** The wordplay here is on the two phrases "to eat one's words" (i.e., to recant what one has said) and "to make someone eat one's sword" (i.e., to force someone to submit). **devised to it:** i.e., provided for it

294. **protest:** declare (as a formal affirmation or vow)

297. **stayed:** stopped; **in a happy hour:** at a fortunate moment

For to strange sores strangely they strain the
    cure.—   265
Come, lady, die to live. This wedding day
Perhaps is but prolonged. Have patience and
    endure.
                ⌜*All but Beatrice and Benedick*⌝ *exit.*

BENEDICK Lady Beatrice, have you wept all this while?
BEATRICE Yea, and I will weep a while longer.   270
BENEDICK I will not desire that.
BEATRICE You have no reason. I do it freely.
BENEDICK Surely I do believe your fair cousin is
    wronged.
BEATRICE Ah, how much might the man deserve of me   275
    that would right her!
BENEDICK Is there any way to show such friendship?
BEATRICE A very even way, but no such friend.
BENEDICK May a man do it?
BEATRICE It is a man's office, but not yours.   280
BENEDICK I do love nothing in the world so well as
    you. Is not that strange?
BEATRICE As strange as the thing I know not. It were as
    possible for me to say I loved nothing so well as you,
    but believe me not, and yet I lie not, I confess   285
    nothing, nor I deny nothing. I am sorry for my
    cousin.
BENEDICK By my sword, Beatrice, thou lovest me!
BEATRICE Do not swear and eat it.
BENEDICK I will swear by it that you love me, and I will   290
    make him eat it that says I love not you.
BEATRICE Will you not eat your word?
BENEDICK With no sauce that can be devised to it. I
    protest I love thee.
BEATRICE Why then, God forgive me.   295
BENEDICK What offense, sweet Beatrice?
BEATRICE You have stayed me in a happy hour. I was
    about to protest I loved you.

307. **I am gone . . . here:** i.e., I have left you even though you are detaining me

315. **approved:** proved to be; **height:** extreme

317-18. **bear her in hand:** i.e., deceive her, lead her on

319. **uncovered:** open, undisguised

323-24. **proper saying:** i.e., a fine story (sarcastic)

327. **undone:** destroyed

329. **counties:** i.e., counts

330. **a goodly count:** a handsome count (with puns on **goodly** as "fine" and on **count** as "story" and as "legal charge"); **Comfect:** comfit or confect, candy

331. **for his sake:** i.e., because of him

BENEDICK   And do it with all thy heart.

BEATRICE   I love you with so much of my heart that 300
none is left to protest.

BENEDICK   Come, bid me do anything for thee.

BEATRICE   Kill Claudio.

BENEDICK   Ha! Not for the wide world.

BEATRICE   You kill me to deny it. Farewell.   305
⌜*She begins to exit.*⌝

BENEDICK   Tarry, sweet Beatrice.

BEATRICE   I am gone, though I am here. There is no
love in you. Nay, I pray you let me go.

BENEDICK   Beatrice—

BEATRICE   In faith, I will go.   310

BENEDICK   We'll be friends first.

BEATRICE   You dare easier be friends with me than
fight with mine enemy.

BENEDICK   Is Claudio thine enemy?

BEATRICE   Is he not approved in the height a villain 315
that hath slandered, scorned, dishonored my kins-
woman? O, that I were a man! What, bear her in
hand until they come to take hands, and then, with
public accusation, uncovered slander, unmitigated
rancor—O God, that I were a man! I would eat his 320
heart in the marketplace.

BENEDICK   Hear me, Beatrice—

BEATRICE   Talk with a man out at a window! A proper
saying.

BENEDICK   Nay, but Beatrice—   325

BEATRICE   Sweet Hero, she is wronged, she is slandered, she is undone.

BENEDICK   Beat—

BEATRICE   Princes and counties! Surely a princely tes-
timony, a goodly count, Count Comfect, a sweet 330
gallant, surely! O, that I were a man for his sake! Or
that I had any friend would be a man for my sake!
But manhood is melted into curtsies, valor into

334. **compliment:** ceremonies of civility or courtesy

335. **trim ones:** i.e., fine, elegant talkers; **He:** i.e., any man; **now:** i.e., these days; **Hercules:** See note to 2.1.250.

336. **swears it:** i.e., swears that it's true

346. **engaged:** committed, pledged

346–47. **challenge him:** i.e., to a duel

348. **render me a dear account:** i.e., pay dearly

4.2 Dogberry ineptly questions Borachio and Conrade about the deception of Claudio and Don Pedro. The Sexton has Borachio and Conrade bound and orders them taken to Leonato.

———————

0 SD. **gowns:** i.e., official black gowns

1. **dissembly:** a mistake for "assembly"

5. **exhibition:** perhaps a mistake for "commission"

compliment, and men are only turned into tongue, and trim ones, too. He is now as valiant as Hercules 335 that only tells a lie and swears it. I cannot be a man with wishing; therefore I will die a woman with grieving.

BENEDICK Tarry, good Beatrice. By this hand, I love thee.   340

BEATRICE Use it for my love some other way than swearing by it.

BENEDICK Think you in your soul the Count Claudio hath wronged Hero?

BEATRICE Yea, as sure as I have a thought or a soul. 345

BENEDICK Enough, I am engaged. I will challenge him. I will kiss your hand, and so I leave you. By this hand, Claudio shall render me a dear account. As you hear of me, so think of me. Go comfort your cousin. I must say she is dead, and so farewell. 350
                                                    ⌐*They exit.*⌐

                              ⌐Scene 2⌐
           Enter the Constables ⌐*Dogberry and Verges,*⌐ *and the*
           Town Clerk, ⌐*or Sexton,*⌐ *in gowns,* ⌐*with the Watch,*
                         Conrade, and⌐ *Borachio.*

⌐DOGBERRY⌐ Is our whole dissembly appeared?

⌐VERGES⌐ O, a stool and a cushion for the Sexton.
                 ⌐*A stool is brought in; the Sexton sits.*⌐

SEXTON Which be the malefactors?

⌐DOGBERRY⌐ Marry, that am I, and my partner.

⌐VERGES⌐ Nay, that's certain, we have the exhibition to 5
examine.

SEXTON But which are the offenders that are to be examined? Let them come before Master Constable.

14. **sirrah:** a term of address to a male social inferior

21. **defend but:** forbid but that

24. **will go near to be:** i.e., will almost be

26. **none:** i.e., nothing of the kind

27. **witty:** clever

28. **go about with:** set to work upon

30. **false:** treacherous, deceitful

33. **both in a tale:** i.e., telling the same story

38. **eftest:** perhaps a mistake for "fastest" or "deftest"

44. **perjury:** a mistake for "treachery"

Hercules. (2.1.250)
From Vincenzo Cartari,
Le vere e noue Imagini . . . (1615).

⌜DOGBERRY⌝ Yea, marry, let them come before me.   10
⌜*Conrade and Borachio are brought forward.*⌝
What is your name, friend?
BORACHIO Borachio.
⌜DOGBERRY⌝ Pray, write down "Borachio."—Yours,
sirrah?
CONRADE I am a gentleman, sir, and my name is   15
Conrade.
⌜DOGBERRY⌝ Write down "Master Gentleman Con-
rade."—Masters, do you serve God?
BORACHIO/CONRADE Yea, sir, we hope.
⌜DOGBERRY⌝ Write down that they hope they serve   20
God; and write God first, for God defend but God
should go before such villains!—Masters, it is
proved already that you are little better than false
knaves, and it will go near to be thought so shortly.
How answer you for yourselves?   25
CONRADE Marry, sir, we say we are none.
⌜DOGBERRY⌝ A marvelous witty fellow, I assure you,
but I will go about with him.—Come you hither,
sirrah, a word in your ear. Sir, I say to you it is
thought you are false knaves.   30
BORACHIO Sir, I say to you we are none.
⌜DOGBERRY⌝ Well, stand aside.—'Fore God, they are
both in a tale. Have you writ down that they are
none?
SEXTON Master constable, you go not the way to   35
examine. You must call forth the watch that are
their accusers.
⌜DOGBERRY⌝ Yea, marry, that's the eftest way.—Let
the watch come forth. Masters, I charge you in the
Prince's name, accuse these men.   40
FIRST WATCHMAN This man said, sir, that Don John, the
Prince's brother, was a villain.
⌜DOGBERRY⌝ Write down Prince John a villain. Why,
this is flat perjury, to call a prince's brother villain!

52. **Flat burglary:** i.e., out-and-out treachery

56. **upon his words:** i.e., on the strength of Borachio's accusation

59. **redemption:** a mistake for "damnation"

65. **refused:** rejected

69. **opinioned:** a mistake for "pinioned" (i.e., bound by the arms)

71. **coxcomb:** i.e., fool (literally, the cap worn by a professional Fool)

72. **God's:** i.e., may God save

74. **naughty:** wicked

76. **suspect:** a mistake for "respect"; **place:** position

77. **years:** i.e., age

A Fool with his coxcomb. (4.2.71)
From Sebastian Brant, *Stultifera nauis* (1570).

BORACHIO Master constable—   45
⌜DOGBERRY⌝ Pray thee, fellow, peace. I do not like thy
    look, I promise thee.
SEXTON, ⌜*to Watch*⌝ What heard you him say else?
⌜SEACOAL⌝ Marry, that he had received a thousand
    ducats of Don John for accusing the Lady Hero   50
    wrongfully.
⌜DOGBERRY⌝ Flat burglary as ever was committed.
⌜VERGES⌝ Yea, by Mass, that it is.
SEXTON What else, fellow?
FIRST WATCHMAN And that Count Claudio did mean,   55
    upon his words, to disgrace Hero before the whole
    assembly, and not marry her.
⌜DOGBERRY, *to Borachio*⌝ O, villain! Thou wilt be con-
    demned into everlasting redemption for this!
SEXTON What else?   60
⌜SEACOAL⌝ This is all.
SEXTON And this is more, masters, than you can deny.
    Prince John is this morning secretly stolen away.
    Hero was in this manner accused, in this very
    manner refused, and upon the grief of this sudden- 65
    ly died.—Master constable, let these men be bound
    and brought to Leonato's. I will go before and show
    him their examination.   ⌜*He exits.*⌝
⌜DOGBERRY⌝ Come, let them be opinioned.
⌜VERGES⌝ Let them be in the hands—   70
⌜CONRADE⌝ Off, coxcomb!
⌜DOGBERRY⌝ God's my life, where's the Sexton? Let
    him write down the Prince's officer "coxcomb."
    Come, bind them.—Thou naughty varlet!
⌜CONRADE⌝ Away! You are an ass, you are an ass!   75
⌜DOGBERRY⌝ Dost thou not suspect my place? Dost
    thou not suspect my years? O, that he were here to
    write me down an ass! But masters, remember that
    I am an ass, though it be not written down, yet
    forget not that I am an ass.—No, thou villain, thou 80

81. **piety:** a mistake, perhaps for "impiety"
85, 86. **go to:** an expression of impatience

"So they sell bullocks." (2.1.192–93)
From Hugh Alley, *A caveat for the city of London* (1598).

art full of piety, as shall be proved upon thee by
good witness. I am a wise fellow and, which is more,
an officer and, which is more, a householder and,
which is more, as pretty a piece of flesh as any is in
Messina, and one that knows the law, go to, and a   85
rich fellow enough, go to, and a fellow that hath had
losses, and one that hath two gowns and everything
handsome about him.—Bring him away.—O, that I
had been writ down an ass!

⌜*They*⌝ *exit.*

MUCH ADO
ABOUT NOTHING

ACT 5

5.1 Leonato and his brother tell Claudio and Don Pedro of Hero's death, and attempt to challenge them to a duel. Benedick succeeds in issuing his challenge to Claudio. Dogberry and the prisoners enter, and Claudio and Don Pedro learn about the trick that was played on them. They also learn that Don John has fled from Messina. Having been convinced of Hero's innocence, Claudio begs Leonato's forgiveness and is told that he must sing an epitaph at Hero's tomb that night. The next morning, he is to marry Leonato's "niece."

---

1 SP. **Leonato's brother:** See note to 1.2.0 SD.

2. **second:** reinforce, assist the effect of

8. **suit with:** correspond with, match

10. **of her:** i.e., in her

12. **Measure his woe:** i.e., let his grief equal

13. **answer . . . strain:** This is primarily a musical metaphor, where one **strain** or phrase of music **answers** another. One could paraphrase as "Let his woe match mine in detail or in intensity."

14. **such a grief for such:** i.e., such a grief matching such another grief

17. **wag:** depart; **hem:** i.e., "h'm" or "ahem" (the word used to represent the sound made when clearing the throat, when expressing doubt, or when coughing to attract attention before speaking)

19. **Patch . . . with proverbs:** mend . . . with proverbial sayings; **drunk:** i.e., stupefied, insensible

20. **With candle-wasters:** i.e., through (the words of) those who read and write late into the night

21. **of him:** i.e., from him

⌐ACT 5⌐

⌐Scene 1⌐
Enter Leonato and his brother.

LEONATO'S BROTHER
If you go on thus, you will kill yourself,
And 'tis not wisdom thus to second grief
Against yourself.

LEONATO   I pray thee, cease thy counsel,
Which falls into mine ears as profitless   5
As water in a sieve. Give not me counsel,
Nor let no comforter delight mine ear
But such a one whose wrongs do suit with mine.
Bring me a father that so loved his child,
Whose joy of her is overwhelmed like mine,   10
And bid him speak of patience.
Measure his woe the length and breadth of mine,
And let it answer every strain for strain,
As thus for thus, and such a grief for such,
In every lineament, branch, shape, and form.   15
If such a one will smile and stroke his beard,
⌐Bid⌐ sorrow wag, cry "hem" when he should
    groan,
Patch grief with proverbs, make misfortune drunk
With candle-wasters, bring him yet to me,   20
And I of him will gather patience.
But there is no such man. For, brother, men

155

25. **passion:** (1) strong emotion; (2) suffering; **which before:** i.e., who earlier

26. **preceptial med'cine:** i.e., medicinal precepts; **to rage:** i.e., to others' anguish or violent pain

28. **Charm:** subdue, control (as with a magic spell)

29. **office:** obligation (said sarcastically)

30. **wring:** twist in anguish, writhe

31. **virtue:** strength, power; **sufficiency:** ability, competency

32. **To be so moral:** i.e., to moralize in that manner

34. **than advertisement:** i.e., than (can be soothed by) instruction or precepts (pronounced **advèrtisement**)

35. **nothing:** not at all

39. **However:** i.e., however much; **writ the style of:** i.e., written in a style worthy of

40. **a push at:** an attack on; **sufferance:** suffering

41. **bend not:** i.e., do not direct; **upon:** against

48. **e'en:** i.e., afternoon (literally, evening)

Can counsel and speak comfort to that grief
Which they themselves not feel, but tasting it,
Their counsel turns to passion, which before   25
Would give preceptial med'cine to rage,
Fetter strong madness in a silken thread,
Charm ache with air and agony with words.
No, no, 'tis all men's office to speak patience
To those that wring under the load of sorrow,   30
But no man's virtue nor sufficiency
To be so moral when he shall endure
The like himself. Therefore give me no counsel.
My griefs cry louder than advertisement.

LEONATO'S BROTHER
Therein do men from children nothing differ.   35

LEONATO
I pray thee, peace. I will be flesh and blood,
For there was never yet philosopher
That could endure the toothache patiently,
However they have writ the style of gods
And made a push at chance and sufferance.   40

LEONATO'S BROTHER
Yet bend not all the harm upon yourself.
Make those that do offend you suffer too.

LEONATO
There thou speak'st reason. Nay, I will do so.
My soul doth tell me Hero is belied,
And that shall Claudio know; so shall the Prince   45
And all of them that thus dishonor her.

Enter Prince and Claudio.

LEONATO'S BROTHER
Here comes the Prince and Claudio hastily.

PRINCE
Good e'en, good e'en.

CLAUDIO   Good day to both of you.

54. **all is one:** i.e., it is all the same; it does not matter

56. **right:** avenge

57. **Some of us:** i.e., Claudio and Don Pedro; **lie low:** i.e., lie prostrate or dead

62. **beshrew:** a mild word for "curse"

63. **your age:** i.e., you as an old man

64. **my . . . sword:** perhaps, I had no plan to use my sword

65. **fleer:** jeer, mock

69. **to thy head:** i.e., to your face

71. **reverence:** state of being venerated (because of age)

73. **trial of a man:** i.e., a trial by combat, a duel

79. **framed:** created

"Enfranchised with a clog." (1.3.31)
From Geoffrey Whitney, *A choice of emblemes* (1586).

LEONATO
Hear you, my lords—   50
PRINCE   We have some haste,
Leonato.
LEONATO
Some haste, my lord! Well, fare you well, my lord.
Are you so hasty now? Well, all is one.
PRINCE
Nay, do not quarrel with us, good old man.   55
LEONATO'S BROTHER
If he could right himself with quarreling,
Some of us would lie low.
CLAUDIO   Who wrongs him?
LEONATO
Marry, thou dost wrong me, thou dissembler, thou.
Nay, never lay thy hand upon thy sword.   60
I fear thee not.
CLAUDIO   Marry, beshrew my hand
If it should give your age such cause of fear.
In faith, my hand meant nothing to my sword.
LEONATO
Tush, tush, man, never fleer and jest at me.   65
I speak not like a dotard nor a fool,
As under privilege of age to brag
What I have done being young, or what would do
Were I not old. Know, Claudio, to thy head,
Thou hast so wronged mine innocent child and me   70
That I am forced to lay my reverence by,
And with gray hairs and bruise of many days
Do challenge thee to trial of a man.
I say thou hast belied mine innocent child.
Thy slander hath gone through and through her   75
   heart,
And she lies buried with her ancestors,
O, in a tomb where never scandal slept,
Save this of hers, framed by thy villainy.

85. **nice fence:** i.e., elegant fencing skills; **practice:** i.e., at swordplay

86. **lustihood:** vigor, robustness

88. **daff:** i.e., doff, discard

92. **Win me and wear me:** proverbial, meaning "defeat me and then boast"

95. **foining fence:** i.e., vigorous swordplay (*To foin* is to pierce or thrust.)

100. **answer:** fight with

102. **apes:** counterfeits; **jacks:** low-born fellows

105. **scruple:** the twenty-fourth part of an ounce (a unit of apothecary weight)

106. **Scambling:** contentious; **outfacing:** i.e., brazen; **fashionmonging:** i.e., foppish

107. **cog:** cheat; or, flatter, wheedle; **deprave:** vilify, disparage

108. **anticly:** i.e., grotesquely dressed; **show outward hideousness:** i.e., look terrifying

CLAUDIO
  My villainy? 80
LEONATO   Thine, Claudio, thine, I say.
PRINCE
  You say not right, old man.
LEONATO   My lord, my lord,
  I'll prove it on his body if he dare,
  Despite his nice fence and his active practice, 85
  His May of youth and bloom of lustihood.
CLAUDIO
  Away! I will not have to do with you.
LEONATO
  Canst thou so daff me? Thou hast killed my child.
  If thou kill'st me, boy, thou shalt kill a man.
LEONATO'S BROTHER
  He shall kill two of us, and men indeed, 90
  But that's no matter. Let him kill one first.
  Win me and wear me! Let him answer me. —
  Come, follow me, boy. Come, sir boy, come, follow
    me.
  Sir boy, I'll whip you from your foining fence, 95
  Nay, as I am a gentleman, I will.
LEONATO Brother—
LEONATO'S BROTHER
  Content yourself. God knows I loved my niece,
  And she is dead, slandered to death by villains
  That dare as well answer a man indeed 100
  As I dare take a serpent by the tongue. —
  Boys, apes, braggarts, jacks, milksops!
LEONATO Brother Anthony—
LEONATO'S BROTHER
  Hold you content. What, man! I know them, yea,
  And what they weigh, even to the utmost scruple— 105
  Scambling, outfacing, fashionmonging boys,
  That lie and cog and flout, deprave and slander,
  Go anticly and show outward hideousness,

114. **meddle:** concern yourself

115. **wake your patience:** perhaps, disturb your peace of mind any further (The line is puzzling. It may be an ironic comment; or some editors have suggested that the text may be corrupt.)

122. **some of us:** i.e., the two of you

128. **had like to have had:** i.e., nearly had

129. **with:** i.e., by

131. **doubt:** suspect

133. **false quarrel:** perhaps, an unfair fight

136. **high-proof:** i.e., impervious, impenetrable; **fain:** gladly

Map of the world with the Antipodes. (2.1.261)
From Macrobius, *In somnium Scipionis* . . . (1492).

162

And speak off half a dozen dang'rous words
How they might hurt their enemies, if they durst, 110
And this is all.
LEONATO But brother Anthony—
LEONATO'S BROTHER Come, 'tis no matter.
Do not you meddle. Let me deal in this.
PRINCE
Gentlemen both, we will not wake your patience. 115
My heart is sorry for your daughter's death,
But, on my honor, she was charged with nothing
But what was true and very full of proof.
LEONATO My lord, my lord—
PRINCE I will not hear you. 120
LEONATO
No? Come, brother, away. I will be heard.
LEONATO'S BROTHER
And shall, or some of us will smart for it.
⌐*Leonato and his brother*⌐ *exit.*

Enter Benedick.

PRINCE
See, see, here comes the man we went to seek.
CLAUDIO Now, signior, what news?
BENEDICK, ⌐*to Prince*⌐ Good day, my lord. 125
PRINCE Welcome, signior. You are almost come to
part almost a fray.
CLAUDIO We had ⌐like⌐ to have had our two noses
snapped off with two old men without teeth.
PRINCE Leonato and his brother. What think'st thou? 130
Had we fought, I doubt we should have been too
young for them.
BENEDICK In a false quarrel there is no true valor. I
came to seek you both.
CLAUDIO We have been up and down to seek thee, for 135
we are high-proof melancholy and would fain have
it beaten away. Wilt thou use thy wit?

141. **beside their wit:** i.e., out of their minds; **draw:** i.e., take out your wit (as you would **draw** your sword)

142. **draw:** Addressed to **minstrels,** this might mean "draw your musical instrument from its case."

145. **What, courage, man:** The word **What** is used as an interjection introducing an exclamation.

146. **care killed a cat:** a common expression; **mettle:** spirit

148. **in the career:** at full speed (a term from tournaments, as are **charge** and **cross**); **an:** if

149. **charge it:** i.e., use it as a weapon

150. **subject:** i.e., person to attack; or, perhaps, topic

151. **staff:** i.e., spear shaft (Using the continuing tournament metaphor, Claudio here says that Benedick's wit has failed him.)

152. **broke 'cross:** i.e., clumsily broken crosswise

153. **By this light:** a mild oath; **changes:** i.e., grows pale

155. **turn his girdle:** Proverbial: "If he be angry, let him turn his girdle." The meaning of the proverb is not known. **girdle:** a belt for carrying a light weapon or keys

159. **make it good:** i.e., enforce my accusation through combat; **how:** i.e., however

160. **Do me right:** i.e., give me satisfaction

161. **protest:** announce, proclaim

164. **meet you:** i.e., in a duel (Don Pedro's response suggests he hears this comment, along with the reference to **good cheer**—i.e., hospitable entertainment—and misinterprets it.)

167. **bid:** invited

(continued)

BENEDICK   It is in my scabbard. Shall I draw it?

PRINCE   Dost thou wear thy wit by thy side?

CLAUDIO   Never any did so, though very many have   140
been beside their wit. I will bid thee draw, as we do
the minstrels: draw to pleasure us.

PRINCE   As I am an honest man, he looks pale. — Art
thou sick, or angry?

CLAUDIO, ⌜to Benedick⌝   What, courage, man! What   145
though care killed a cat? Thou hast mettle enough
in thee to kill care.

BENEDICK   Sir, I shall meet your wit in the career, an
you charge it against me. I pray you, choose another
subject.   150

CLAUDIO, ⌜to Prince⌝   Nay, then, give him another staff.
This last was broke 'cross.

PRINCE   By this light, he changes more and more. I
think he be angry indeed.

CLAUDIO   If he be, he knows how to turn his girdle.   155

BENEDICK   Shall I speak a word in your ear?

CLAUDIO   God bless me from a challenge!

BENEDICK, ⌜aside to Claudio⌝   You are a villain. I jest
not. I will make it good how you dare, with what you
dare, and when you dare. Do me right, or I will   160
protest your cowardice. You have killed a sweet
lady, and her death shall fall heavy on you. Let me
hear from you.

CLAUDIO   Well, I will meet you, so I may have good
cheer.   165

PRINCE   What, a feast, a feast?

CLAUDIO   I' faith, I thank him. He hath bid me to a
calf's head and a capon, the which if I do not carve
most curiously, say my knife's naught. Shall I not
find a woodcock too?   170

BENEDICK   Sir, your wit ambles well; it goes easily.

PRINCE   I'll tell thee how Beatrice praised thy wit the
other day. I said thou hadst a fine wit. "True," said

168, 170. **calf's head, capon, woodcock:** Each of these could be an item at a **feast** (dishes that Claudio is ready to **carve**), but each also has a symbolic, insulting meaning: **calf's head** and **woodcock** mean "simpleton"; **capon** (a castrated cock) means "eunuch."

169. **curiously:** elaborately, exquisitely; **naught:** worthless

174. **fine:** extremely narrow

176. **Just:** exactly

178. **wise gentleman:** perhaps a sarcastic name for a fool

179. **tongues:** i.e., ability to speak many languages

181. **forswore:** repudiated, renounced

183. **transshape:** alter the shape of

185. **proper'st:** finest, handsomest

188. **an if:** i.e., if

191–92. **God saw him . . . in the garden:** In the book of Genesis, after Adam eats the apple forbidden him in the Garden of Eden, he "and his wife hid themselves from the presence of the Lord God among the trees of the garden" (3.8).

193–96. **the savage bull's . . . married man:** a reference to 1.1.256–62.

198. **gossip-like:** A **gossip** was a gossiping or tattling woman. **humor:** mood

199. **braggarts . . . blades:** a reference to the way braggarts damage their own weapons and then brag that they broke them in a fight

201. **courtesies:** kindnesses

205. **meet:** i.e., in a duel; **peace be with him:** a phrase used as a greeting or, as here, a farewell

she, "a fine little one." "No," said I, "a great wit."
"Right," says she, "a great gross one." "Nay," said I,   175
"a good wit." "Just," said she, "it hurts nobody."
"Nay," said I, "the gentleman is wise." "Certain,"
said she, "a wise gentleman." "Nay," said I, "he
hath the tongues." "That I believe," said she, "for he
swore a thing to me on Monday night which he   180
forswore on Tuesday morning; there's a double
tongue, there's two tongues." Thus did she an hour
together transshape thy particular virtues. Yet at
last she concluded with a sigh, thou wast the
proper'st man in Italy.   185

CLAUDIO For the which she wept heartily and said she
cared not.

PRINCE Yea, that she did. But yet for all that, an if she
did not hate him deadly, she would love him
dearly. The old man's daughter told us all.   190

CLAUDIO All, all. And, moreover, God saw him when
he was hid in the garden.

PRINCE But when shall we set the savage bull's horns
on the sensible Benedick's head?

CLAUDIO Yea, and text underneath: "Here dwells Ben-   195
edick, the married man"?

BENEDICK Fare you well, boy. You know my mind. I
will leave you now to your gossip-like humor. You
break jests as braggarts do their blades, which, God
be thanked, hurt not.—My lord, for your many   200
courtesies I thank you. I must discontinue your
company. Your brother the Bastard is fled from
Messina. You have among you killed a sweet and
innocent lady. For my Lord Lackbeard there, he and
I shall meet, and till then peace be with him.   205

⌜*Benedick exits.*⌝

PRINCE He is in earnest.

CLAUDIO In most profound earnest, and, I'll warrant
you, for the love of Beatrice.

212. **leaves off his wit:** i.e., forgets to wear his intelligence

213–14. **He is . . . man:** These lines have been variously (and unsatisfactorily) explained. **to an ape:** perhaps, in the eyes of the ape; or, in comparison to an ape; **doctor:** man of learning

215. **soft you:** an exclamation meaning "wait a minute"; **Pluck up:** take courage

216. **sad:** serious

218. **she shall . . . balance:** The image is of Justice with her balance scales; since **reasons** was pronounced like *raisins,* there is a secondary image of a vendor weighing fruit to sell.

219. **an:** i.e., if; **once:** i.e., in a word

221. **bound:** in bonds, tied up

223. **Hearken after:** i.e., ask about

227. **slanders:** i.e., slanderers

228. **verified:** asserted

232. **committed:** i.e., being sent to prison

232–33. **lay to their charge:** i.e., charge them with

234. **division:** i.e., way of enumerating the parts

235. **meaning:** idea, topic; **suited:** perhaps, set out in a sequence; or, perhaps, dressed (in a variety of clothes)

237–38. **bound to your answer:** i.e., tied up, compelled, and on your way to make your legal defense (a triple pun on **bound**)

238. **cunning:** clever

241. **Do you hear me:** i.e., listen to me

PRINCE   And hath challenged thee?

CLAUDIO   Most sincerely.   210

PRINCE   What a pretty thing man is when he goes in his
doublet and hose and leaves off his wit!

CLAUDIO   He is then a giant to an ape; but then is an ape
a doctor to such a man.

PRINCE   But soft you, let me be. Pluck up, my heart,   215
and be sad. Did he not say my brother was fled?

Enter Constables ⌐*Dogberry and Verges, and the Watch,*
with⌐ *Conrade and Borachio.*

⌐DOGBERRY⌐   Come you, sir. If justice cannot tame you,
she shall ne'er weigh more reasons in her balance.
Nay, an you be a cursing hypocrite once, you must
be looked to.   220

PRINCE   How now, two of my brother's men bound?
Borachio one!

CLAUDIO   Hearken after their offense, my lord.

PRINCE   Officers, what offense have these men done?

⌐DOGBERRY⌐   Marry, sir, they have committed false   225
report; moreover, they have spoken untruths; sec-
ondarily, they are slanders; sixth and lastly, they
have belied a lady; thirdly, they have verified unjust
things; and, to conclude, they are lying knaves.

PRINCE   First, I ask thee what they have done; thirdly, I   230
ask thee what's their offense; sixth and lastly, why
they are committed; and, to conclude, what you lay
to their charge.

CLAUDIO   Rightly reasoned, and in his own division;
and, by my troth, there's one meaning well suited.   235

PRINCE, ⌐*to Borachio and Conrade*⌐   Who have you of-
fended, masters, that you are thus bound to your
answer? This learned constable is too cunning to be
understood. What's your offense?

BORACHIO   Sweet prince, let me go no farther to mine   240
answer. Do you hear me, and let this count kill me.

246. **incensed:** incited
247. **orchard:** formal garden
250. **seal:** i.e., guarantee (the **record** of my villainy) to be true
258-59. **the practice of it:** i.e., putting it in practice
260. **framed:** created, constructed
261. **upon:** i.e., because of, as a result of
263. **semblance:** form, image
264. **plaintiffs:** a mistake for "defendants" or "prisoners"
265. **reformed:** a mistake for "informed"

I have deceived even your very eyes. What your
wisdoms could not discover, these shallow fools
have brought to light, who in the night overheard
me confessing to this man how Don John your   245
brother incensed me to slander the Lady Hero, how
you were brought into the orchard and saw me
court Margaret in Hero's garments, how you dis-
graced her when you should marry her. My villainy
they have upon record, which I had rather seal with   250
my death than repeat over to my shame. The lady is
dead upon mine and my master's false accusation.
And, briefly, I desire nothing but the reward of a
villain.

PRINCE, ⌜to Claudio⌝
Runs not this speech like iron through your blood?   255

CLAUDIO
I have drunk poison whiles he uttered it.

PRINCE, ⌜to Borachio⌝
But did my brother set thee on to this?

BORACHIO   Yea, and paid me richly for the practice of
it.

PRINCE
He is composed and framed of treachery,   260
And fled he is upon this villainy.

CLAUDIO
Sweet Hero, now thy image doth appear
In the rare semblance that I loved it first.

⌜DOGBERRY⌝   Come, bring away the plaintiffs. By this
time our sexton hath reformed Signior Leonato of   265
the matter. And, masters, do not forget to specify,
when time and place shall serve, that I am an ass.

⌜VERGES⌝   Here, here comes Master Signior Leonato,
and the Sexton too.

Enter Leonato, his brother, and the Sexton.

277. **beliest:** tell lies about

282. **bravely:** (1) courageously; (2) splendidly

283. **pray:** i.e., beg

285. **Impose me to:** subject me to, make me undergo; **invention:** inventiveness

294. **Possess:** inform

296. **aught:** at all; **invention:** composing, devising (here, the writing of a poem or song)

297. **Hang her:** i.e., hang for her

LEONATO
  Which is the villain? Let me see his eyes,   270
  That, when I note another man like him,
  I may avoid him. Which of these is he?
BORACHIO
  If you would know your wronger, look on me.
LEONATO
  Art thou the slave that with thy breath hast killed
  Mine innocent child?   275
BORACHIO   Yea, even I alone.
LEONATO
  No, not so, villain, thou beliest thyself.
  Here stand a pair of honorable men—
  A third is fled—that had a hand in it.—
  I thank you, princes, for my daughter's death.   280
  Record it with your high and worthy deeds.
  'Twas bravely done, if you bethink you of it.
CLAUDIO
  I know not how to pray your patience,
  Yet I must speak. Choose your revenge yourself.
  Impose me to what penance your invention   285
  Can lay upon my sin. Yet sinned I not
  But in mistaking.
PRINCE   By my soul, nor I,
  And yet to satisfy this good old man
  I would bend under any heavy weight   290
  That he'll enjoin me to.
LEONATO
  I cannot bid you bid my daughter live—
  That were impossible—but, I pray you both,
  Possess the people in Messina here
  How innocent she died. And if your love   295
  Can labor aught in sad invention,
  Hang her an epitaph upon her tomb
  And sing it to her bones. Sing it tonight.
  Tomorrow morning come you to my house,

301. **yet:** nevertheless

311. **naughty:** wicked

313. **packed in:** i.e., an accomplice to

318. **by her:** i.e., of her

320. **under white and black:** i.e., written down; **plaintiff:** a mistake for "offender"

325–26. **the which he hath used:** i.e., a habit which he has practiced

333. **God save the foundation:** i.e., God bless the founder (said at the doors of charitable religious houses)

"And sigh away Sundays." (1.1.197–98)
From *The whole psalmes in foure partes* . . . (1563).

174

And since you could not be my son-in-law,   300
Be yet my nephew. My brother hath a daughter,
Almost the copy of my child that's dead,
And she alone is heir to both of us.
Give her the right you should have giv'n her cousin,
And so dies my revenge.   305

CLAUDIO   O, noble sir!
Your overkindness doth wring tears from me.
I do embrace your offer and dispose
For henceforth of poor Claudio.

LEONATO
Tomorrow then I will expect your coming.   310
Tonight I take my leave. This naughty man
Shall face to face be brought to Margaret,
Who I believe was packed in all this wrong,
Hired to it by your brother.

BORACHIO   No, by my soul, she was not,   315
Nor knew not what she did when she spoke to me,
But always hath been just and virtuous
In anything that I do know by her.

⌐DOGBERRY, *to Leonato*⌐ Moreover, sir, which indeed is
not under white and black, this plaintiff here, the   320
offender, did call me ass. I beseech you, let it be
remembered in his punishment. And also the watch
heard them talk of one Deformed. They say he
wears a key in his ear and a lock hanging by it and
borrows money in God's name, the which he hath   325
used so long and never paid that now men grow
hardhearted and will lend nothing for God's sake.
Pray you, examine him upon that point.

LEONATO   I thank thee for thy care and honest pains.

⌐DOGBERRY⌐   Your Worship speaks like a most thankful   330
and reverent youth, and I praise God for you.

LEONATO, ⌐*giving him money*⌐ There's for thy pains.

⌐DOGBERRY⌐   God save the foundation.

340. **give you leave:** a mistake for "ask your leave"
341. **prohibit:** a mistake for "permit" or "foster"
349. **lewd:** base, disreputable

5.2 Benedick tells Beatrice that he has challenged Claudio. They are summoned to Leonato's house with the news that Hero's innocence has been proved.

––––––––

2. **to the speech of:** i.e., to speak with
7. **come over it:** Benedick plays with the fact that **style** sounds like "stile" (a set of steps built over a fence). **Come over it** can thus mean (1) write in a more elegant style; and (2) climb over the stile.
9. **come over me:** i.e., make love to me
10. **keep below stairs:** remain in the servants' quarters (There seems to be an implied pun here on **mistress** as "the lady of the house"—and therefore not "below stairs"—and as "a woman with a lover.")

LEONATO Go, I discharge thee of thy prisoner, and I
 thank thee.   335
⌈DOGBERRY⌉ I leave an arrant knave with your Wor-
 ship, which I beseech your Worship to correct
 yourself, for the example of others. God keep your
 Worship! I wish your Worship well. God restore you
 to health. I humbly give you leave to depart, and if a 340
 merry meeting may be wished, God prohibit it.—
 Come, neighbor.   ⌈*Dogberry and Verges exit.*⌉
LEONATO
Until tomorrow morning, lords, farewell.
LEONATO'S BROTHER
Farewell, my lords. We look for you tomorrow.
PRINCE
We will not fail.   345
CLAUDIO   Tonight I'll mourn with Hero.
LEONATO, ⌈*to Watch*⌉
Bring you these fellows on.—We'll talk with
 Margaret,
How her acquaintance grew with this lewd fellow.
                                        They exit.

⌈Scene 2⌉
Enter Benedick and Margaret.

BENEDICK Pray thee, sweet Mistress Margaret, deserve
 well at my hands by helping me to the speech of
 Beatrice.
MARGARET Will you then write me a sonnet in praise
 of my beauty?   5
BENEDICK In so high a style, Margaret, that no man
 living shall come over it, for in most comely truth
 thou deservest it.
MARGARET To have no man come over me? Why, shall I
 always keep below stairs?   10

16–17. **I give thee the bucklers:** i.e., I give up (in this wit combat) **bucklers:** small shields used in swordfighting (See page 180.) The double entendre on **swords** and **bucklers** that begins in line 18 continues with **pikes, vice,** and **maids.**

21. **pikes:** spikes in the center of bucklers; **vice:** i.e., vise (a clamp used in carpentry or metalworking)

26–29. **The god of love:** This stanza is the beginning of a popular old song.

30. **Leander:** in Greek mythology, a famous lover who drowned swimming across the Hellespont to see his sweetheart (See page 188 and longer note to 4.1.87, especially the final paragraph, page 204.)

31. **Troilus:** famed for his love for Cressida, whose uncle Pandarus made their affair possible

32. **quondam:** bygone, former; **carpetmongers:** i.e., pretend lovers (The word seems to have been constructed by analogy with "carpet knight," a man knighted not on the battlefield but at court, and thus a pretend warrior. The word means literally "sellers of carpets.")

33. **even:** smooth

37. **an innocent:** a childish, a silly

38. **hard:** (1) harsh, unpleasant sounding; (2) referring to the unpleasant idea of cuckoldry

40–41. **under a rhyming planet:** i.e., under the influence of a planet that bestows poetic gifts

41. **festival:** joyful, glad

BENEDICK   Thy wit is as quick as the greyhound's mouth; it catches.

MARGARET   And yours as blunt as the fencer's foils, which hit but hurt not.

BENEDICK   A most manly wit, Margaret; it will not hurt   15
a woman. And so, I pray thee, call Beatrice. I give thee the bucklers.

MARGARET   Give us the swords; we have bucklers of our own.

BENEDICK   If you use them, Margaret, you must put in   20
the pikes with a vice, and they are dangerous weapons for maids.

MARGARET   Well, I will call Beatrice to you, who I think hath legs.

BENEDICK   And therefore will come.   25

Margaret exits.

⌜*Sings*⌝   *The god of love*
                That sits above,
        And knows me, and knows me,
            How pitiful I deserve—

I mean in singing. But in loving, Leander the good   30
swimmer, Troilus the first employer of panders, and a whole book full of these quondam carpetmon-gers, whose names yet run smoothly in the even road of a blank verse, why, they were never so truly turned over and over as my poor self in love. Marry,   35
I cannot show it in rhyme. I have tried. I can find out no rhyme to "lady" but "baby"—an innocent rhyme; for "scorn," "horn"—a hard rhyme; for "school," "fool"—a babbling rhyme; very ominous endings. No, I was not born under a rhyming   40
planet, nor I cannot woo in festival terms.

Enter Beatrice.

Sweet Beatrice, wouldst thou come when I called thee?

47. **that I came:** i.e., what I came for

55. **frighted:** i.e., frightened; **his:** i.e., its

58–59. **subscribe him:** write him down as

60. **parts:** attributes

63. **politic:** (1) judiciously governed; (2) cunning

65. **suffer:** (1) experience; (2) undergo the pains of

66. **epithet:** term, expression; **do suffer:** am subjected to

72. **wise:** clever (In Beatrice's response, **wise** has its usual meaning.)

73. **It appears not:** i.e., your wisdom does not reveal itself

76. **instance:** i.e., saying (literally, example or case)

77. **good neighbors:** Proverbial: "He has ill [i.e., bad] neighbors who is fain to praise himself."

78–79. **live no longer in monument:** i.e., be memorialized no longer

79. **bell:** i.e., church bell tolled for funerals

A buckler. (5.2.17)
From Louis de Gaya, *A treatise of the arms* . . . (1678).

BEATRICE   Yea, signior, and depart when you bid me.

BENEDICK   O, stay but till then!   45

BEATRICE   "Then" is spoken. Fare you well now. And
yet, ere I go, let me go with that I came, which is,
with knowing what hath passed between you and
Claudio.

BENEDICK   Only foul words, and thereupon I will kiss   50
thee.

BEATRICE   Foul words is but foul wind, and foul wind is
but foul breath, and foul breath is noisome. Therefore I will depart unkissed.

BENEDICK   Thou hast frighted the word out of his right   55
sense, so forcible is thy wit. But I must tell thee
plainly, Claudio undergoes my challenge, and either
I must shortly hear from him, or I will subscribe
him a coward. And I pray thee now tell me, for
which of my bad parts didst thou first fall in love   60
with me?

BEATRICE   For them all together, which maintained so
politic a state of evil that they will not admit any
good part to intermingle with them. But for which
of my good parts did you first suffer love for me?   65

BENEDICK   Suffer love! A good epithet. I do suffer love
indeed, for I love thee against my will.

BEATRICE   In spite of your heart, I think. Alas, poor
heart, if you spite it for my sake, I will spite it for
yours, for I will never love that which my friend   70
hates.

BENEDICK   Thou and I are too wise to woo peaceably.

BEATRICE   It appears not in this confession. There's not
one wise man among twenty that will praise himself.   75

BENEDICK   An old, an old instance, Beatrice, that lived
in the time of good neighbors. If a man do not erect
in this age his own tomb ere he dies, he shall live no
longer in monument than the bell rings and the
widow weeps.   80

82. **Question:** perhaps, a good question (and here is the answer); **clamor:** i.e., the tolling of the bell

83. **quarter:** i.e., quarter of an hour; **rheum:** i.e., weeping

84. **Don Worm, his conscience:** The traditional linking of pangs of conscience with a gnawing worm may derive from the biblical descriptions of the damned as those whose "worm shall not die, neither shall their fire be quenched" (Isaiah 66.24, echoed at Mark 9.44, 46, 48).

90. **ill:** badly

93. **mend:** get better

96. **old coil:** i.e., all kinds of turmoil

98. **abused:** deceived

99. **presently:** at once

101. **die:** (1) die for love; (2) experience sexual orgasm

5.3 Claudio appears at Leonato's family tomb, has a song sung for Hero, and hangs a scroll on the tomb.

BEATRICE   And how long is that, think you?

BENEDICK   Question: why, an hour in clamor and a
quarter in rheum. Therefore is it most expedient for
the wise, if Don Worm, his conscience, find no
impediment to the contrary, to be the trumpet of   85
his own virtues, as I am to myself. So much for
praising myself, who, I myself will bear witness, is
praiseworthy. And now tell me, how doth your
cousin?

BEATRICE   Very ill.   90

BENEDICK   And how do you?

BEATRICE   Very ill, too.

BENEDICK   Serve God, love me, and mend. There will I
leave you too, for here comes one in haste.

Enter Ursula.

URSULA   Madam, you must come to your uncle. Yon-   95
der's old coil at home. It is proved my Lady Hero
hath been falsely accused, the Prince and Claudio
mightily abused, and Don John is the author of all,
who is fled and gone. Will you come presently?
⌐*Ursula exits.*⌐

BEATRICE   Will you go hear this news, signior?   100

BENEDICK   I will live in thy heart, die in thy lap, and be
buried in thy eyes—and, moreover, I will go with
thee to thy uncle's.

⌐*They*⌐ *exit.*

⌐Scene 3⌐
Enter Claudio, Prince, and three or four ⌐*Lords*⌐ *with
tapers,* ⌐*and Musicians.*⌐

CLAUDIO   Is this the monument of Leonato?

⌐FIRST⌐ LORD   It is, my lord.

5. **guerdon:** recompense

12. **goddess of the night:** Diana, goddess of the moon and of chastity (hence the reference to Hero as Diana's **virgin knight**)

18. **Heavily:** sadly, mournfully

19. **yawn:** i.e., open

20. **Till death be utterèd:** The verb *to utter* could mean both "to express" and "to vanquish." This much-debated line might therefore mean "till Hero's death be fully expressed" or "until death be vanquished."

24. **morrow:** morning

25. **have preyed:** i.e., have finished their preying

26. **the wheels of Phoebus:** i.e., the chariot of **Phoebus,** god of the sun

29. **several:** separate

Phoebus in his chariot. (5.3.26)
From Hyginus, *Fabularum liber* (1549).

⌐CLAUDIO, *reading an*⌐ *Epitaph.*

> *Done to death by slanderous tongues*
> *Was the Hero that here lies.*
> *Death, in guerdon of her wrongs,*   5
> *Gives her fame which never dies.*
> *So the life that died with shame*
> *Lives in death with glorious fame.*
>   ⌐*He hangs up the scroll.*⌐

Hang thou there upon the tomb,
Praising her when I am ⌐dumb.⌐   10
Now music, sound, and sing your solemn hymn.

Song

> *Pardon, goddess of the night,*
> *Those that slew thy virgin knight,*
> *For the which with songs of woe,*
> *Round about her tomb they go,*   15
> *Midnight, assist our moan.*
> *Help us to sigh and groan*
> *Heavily, heavily.*
> *Graves, yawn and yield your dead,*
> *Till death be utterèd,*   20
> *Heavily, heavily.*

⌐CLAUDIO⌐
Now, unto thy bones, goodnight.
Yearly will I do this rite.
PRINCE
Good morrow, masters. Put your torches out.
    The wolves have preyed, and look, the gentle day   25
Before the wheels of Phoebus, round about
    Dapples the drowsy east with spots of gray.
Thanks to you all, and leave us. Fare you well.
CLAUDIO
Good morrow, masters. Each his several way.
                          ⌐*Lords and Musicians exit.*⌐

30. **weeds:** clothing

32. **Hymen:** god of marriage (See page 196.); **issue:** result; **speed 's:** i.e., speed us, favor us

5.4 Claudio and Don Pedro appear for the second wedding. The women enter masked. When Claudio takes the hand of Leonato's "niece," agreeing to marry her, she unmasks and he learns that she is Hero. Benedick and Beatrice agree to marry, but only out of pity for each other. Love poems each has written to the other are produced to prove that they do, in fact, love each other. Claudio is forgiven by all, and a double wedding is set to follow the closing dance.

---

3. **Upon:** i.e., because of; **debated:** discussed

5. **against her will:** perhaps, unintentionally (The phrase more commonly means "unwillingly.")

6. **question:** investigation

7. **sorts:** turn out

8. **else:** otherwise; **by faith:** i.e., through my promise

9. **call . . . to a reckoning:** make . . . give an account of himself

14. **office:** part

PRINCE

    Come, let us hence, and put on other weeds,   30
    And then to Leonato's we will go.

CLAUDIO

    And Hymen now with luckier issue speed 's,
    Than this for whom we rendered up this woe.

They exit.

⌜Scene 4⌝
Enter Leonato, Benedick, ⌜Beatrice,⌝ Margaret, Ursula,
⌜Leonato's brother,⌝ Friar, Hero.

FRIAR

    Did I not tell you she was innocent?

LEONATO

    So are the Prince and Claudio, who accused her
    Upon the error that you heard debated.
    But Margaret was in some fault for this,
    Although against her will, as it appears   5
    In the true course of all the question.

LEONATO'S BROTHER

    Well, I am glad that all things sorts so well.

BENEDICK

    And so am I, being else by faith enforced
    To call young Claudio to a reckoning for it.

LEONATO

    Well, daughter, and you gentlewomen all,   10
    Withdraw into a chamber by yourselves,
    And when I send for you, come hither masked.
    The Prince and Claudio promised by this hour
    To visit me.—You know your office, brother.
    You must be father to your brother's daughter,   15
    And give her to young Claudio.   *The ladies exit.*

17. **confirmed countenance:** i.e., controlled facial expression

18. **pains:** i.e., help

20. **undo:** (1) unbind; (2) destroy

28. **for:** i.e., as for; **my will is:** i.e., my desire is that

37. **attend:** await, wait upon; **yet:** still

39. **hold:** i.e., not change; **Ethiope:** Ethiopian, or anyone with black skin (Dark hair and skin were not considered beautiful in Elizabethan England.)

Leander swimming the Hellespont. (5.2.30)
From Musaeus, [*Hero and Leander*] (1538).

LEONATO'S BROTHER
  Which I will do with confirmed countenance.
BENEDICK
  Friar, I must entreat your pains, I think.
FRIAR   To do what, signior?
BENEDICK
  To bind me, or undo me, one of them.—   20
  Signior Leonato, truth it is, good signior,
  Your niece regards me with an eye of favor.
LEONATO
  That eye my daughter lent her; 'tis most true.
BENEDICK
  And I do with an eye of love requite her.
LEONATO
  The sight whereof I think you had from me,   25
  From Claudio, and the Prince. But what's your will?
BENEDICK
  Your answer, sir, is enigmatical.
  But for my will, my will is your goodwill
  May stand with ours, this day to be conjoined
  In the state of honorable marriage—   30
  In which, good friar, I shall desire your help.
LEONATO
  My heart is with your liking.
FRIAR   And my help.
  Here comes the Prince and Claudio.

  Enter Prince, and Claudio, and two or three other.

PRINCE   Good morrow to this fair assembly.   35
LEONATO
  Good morrow, prince; good morrow, Claudio.
  We here attend you. Are you yet determined
  Today to marry with my brother's daughter?
CLAUDIO
  I'll hold my mind were she an Ethiope.

44. **savage bull:** a reference to 1.1.256.

45. **horns:** (1) of the bull; (2) of the cuckold

46. **Europa:** Europe

47–48. **Europa . . . love:** Jove, king of the Roman gods, fell in love with a girl named Europa, transformed himself into a bull and, when she climbed on his back, carried her off to Crete. (See page 192.)

50. **leapt:** mounted, mated with

51. **got:** begot

53. **I owe you:** i.e., I'll pay you back; **reck'nings:** i.e., matters to be dealt with

55 SP. **Leonato:** Most editions change this speech prefix, since Leonato's brother had agreed to act as the "niece's" father. However, since the "niece" is really Hero, one can argue that Leonato changes his mind, or that he forgets himself and resumes his fatherly role.

60. **like of:** i.e., like

LEONATO
Call her forth, brother. Here's the Friar ready.   40
                    ⌜*Leonato's brother exits.*⌝
PRINCE
Good morrow, Benedick. Why, what's the matter
That you have such a February face,
So full of frost, of storm, and cloudiness?
CLAUDIO
I think he thinks upon the savage bull.
Tush, fear not, man. We'll tip thy horns with gold,   45
And all Europa shall rejoice at thee,
As once Europa did at lusty Jove
When he would play the noble beast in love.
BENEDICK
Bull Jove, sir, had an amiable low,
And some such strange bull leapt your father's cow   50
And got a calf in that same noble feat
Much like to you, for you have just his bleat.
CLAUDIO
For this I owe you. Here comes other reck'nings.

Enter ⌜*Leonato's*⌝ *brother, Hero, Beatrice, Margaret,*
Ursula, ⌜*the ladies masked.*⌝

Which is the lady I must seize upon?
LEONATO
This same is she, and I do give you her.   55
CLAUDIO
Why, then, she's mine.—Sweet, let me see your face.
LEONATO
No, that you shall not till you take her hand
Before this friar and swear to marry her.
CLAUDIO, ⌜*to Hero*⌝
Give me your hand before this holy friar.
                              ⌜*They take hands.*⌝
I am your husband, if you like of me.   60

68. **but whiles:** only as long as

69. **amazement:** a strong word, meaning "bewilderment," "complete confusion" (as if lost in a maze); **qualify:** mitigate, calm, pacify

70. **after that:** i.e., after

71. **largely:** fully, at length

72. **let wonder seem familiar:** i.e., treat these miraculous events as if they were everyday happenings

73. **let us presently:** i.e., let us go at once

74. **Soft and fair:** i.e., wait a moment

Europa and "Bull Jove." (5.4.46–48)
From Gabriele Simeoni, *La vita . . . d'Ouidio* (1559).

HERO
  And when I lived, I was your other wife,
  And when you loved, you were my other husband.
                                  ⌜*She unmasks.*⌝
CLAUDIO
  Another Hero!
HERO   Nothing certainer.
  One Hero died defiled, but I do live,   65
  And surely as I live, I am a maid.
PRINCE
  The former Hero! Hero that is dead!
LEONATO
  She died, my lord, but whiles her slander lived.
FRIAR
  All this amazement can I qualify,
  When after that the holy rites are ended,   70
  I'll tell you largely of fair Hero's death.
  Meantime let wonder seem familiar,
  And to the chapel let us presently.
BENEDICK
  Soft and fair, friar.—Which is Beatrice?
BEATRICE, ⌜*unmasking*⌝
  I answer to that name. What is your will?   75
BENEDICK
  Do not you love me?
BEATRICE   Why no, no more than reason.
BENEDICK
  Why then, your uncle and the Prince and Claudio
  Have been deceived. They swore you did.
BEATRICE
  Do not you love me?   80
BENEDICK   Troth, no, no more than reason.
BEATRICE
  Why then, my cousin, Margaret, and Ursula
  Are much deceived, for they did swear you did.

86. **'Tis no such matter:** i.e., it isn't true

88. **cousin:** i.e., niece

91. **halting:** lame, limping; **of . . . brain:** i.e., purely or entirely from his own brain

96. **hands:** i.e., handwriting

96–97. **against our hearts:** i.e., as evidence to prove our hearts guilty (of love)

97, 99. **by this light, by this good day:** mild oaths

101. **consumption:** wasting disease (i.e., lovesickness)

102. **stop your mouth:** i.e., compel you to be silent (literally, with a gag or muzzle; here, with a kiss)

104. **a college:** i.e., an (entire) company

105. **wit-crackers:** i.e., those who make sarcastic remarks; **flout:** mock, jeer; **humor:** inclination, state of mind

106. **care for:** i.e., care about, am bothered by

107. **brains:** i.e., witticisms

109. **do purpose:** intend

109–10. **to any purpose:** i.e., of any use

BENEDICK
They swore that you were almost sick for me.
BEATRICE
They swore that you were well-nigh dead for me.   85
BENEDICK
'Tis no such matter. Then you do not love me?
BEATRICE
No, truly, but in friendly recompense.
LEONATO
Come, cousin, I am sure you love the gentleman.
CLAUDIO
And I'll be sworn upon 't that he loves her,
For here's a paper written in his hand,   90
A halting sonnet of his own pure brain,
Fashioned to Beatrice.   ⌜*He shows a paper.*⌝
HERO   And here's another,
Writ in my cousin's hand, stol'n from her pocket,
Containing her affection unto Benedick.   95
                         ⌜*She shows a paper.*⌝
BENEDICK   A miracle! Here's our own hands against
    our hearts. Come, I will have thee, but by this light
    I take thee for pity.
BEATRICE   I would not deny you, but by this good day, I
    yield upon great persuasion, and partly to save your 100
    life, for I was told you were in a consumption.
⌜BENEDICK⌝   Peace! I will stop your mouth.
                                    ⌜*They kiss.*⌝
PRINCE
How dost thou, Benedick, the married man?
BENEDICK   I'll tell thee what, prince: a college of
    wit-crackers cannot flout me out of my humor.   105
    Dost thou think I care for a satire or an epigram?
    No. If a man will be beaten with brains, he shall
    wear nothing handsome about him. In brief, since I
    do purpose to marry, I will think nothing to any
    purpose that the world can say against it, and   110

114. **like:** likely

116. **denied:** i.e., refused to marry

118. **single:** (1) individual; (2) unmarried; (3) weak, feeble; **double-dealer:** (1) someone no longer single, but part of a couple; (2) one who acts duplicitously

118–19. **out of question:** i.e., without any doubt

119–20. **look exceeding narrowly to thee:** i.e., watch you extremely closely

125. **of my word:** i.e., on my word

127. **staff:** (1) i.e., wood or ivory rod carried as a symbol of a position's authority (hence, here, a high-ranking man, like Don Pedro); **reverend:** worthy of veneration

127–28. **tipped with horn:** (1) with a tip of ivory or other animal horn; (2) wearing the cuckold's horns (See longer note to 1.1.194–95, page 199.)

132. **brave:** splendid

Hymen, god of marriage. (5.3.32)
From Vincenzo Cartari, *Imagines deorum* . . . (1581).

therefore never flout at me for what I have said
against it. For man is a giddy thing, and this is my
conclusion.—For thy part, Claudio, I did think to
have beaten thee, but in that thou art like to be my
kinsman, live unbruised, and love my cousin.   115
CLAUDIO   I had well hoped thou wouldst have denied
Beatrice, that I might have cudgeled thee out of thy
single life, to make thee a double-dealer, which out
of question thou wilt be, if my cousin do not look
exceeding narrowly to thee.   120
BENEDICK   Come, come, we are friends. Let's have a
dance ere we are married, that we may lighten our
own hearts and our wives' heels.
LEONATO   We'll have dancing afterward.
BENEDICK   First, of my word! Therefore play, music.—   125
Prince, thou art sad. Get thee a wife, get thee a wife.
There is no staff more reverend than one tipped
with horn.

Enter Messenger.

MESSENGER, ⌈*to Prince*⌉
My lord, your brother John is ta'en in flight,
And brought with armed men back to Messina.   130
BENEDICK, ⌈*to Prince*⌉   Think not on him till tomorrow.
I'll devise thee brave punishments for him.—Strike
up, pipers!   ⌈*Music plays. They*⌉ *dance.*
⌈*They exit.*⌉

Longer Notes

1.1.0 SD. Enter Leonato: In the early printed texts of the play, Leonato's wife, Innogen, is listed here and in the opening entrance for Act 2, among the characters entering. She is given no speeches, is never spoken to, and is not listed in later scenes—for example, at Hero's wedding. It is assumed by editors that Shakespeare decided not to develop this character, though some recent scholars have argued that she should be a silent presence in the play. Her presence in this opening scene when Benedick jokes about her possible adultery, and her silence in the wedding scene as Hero is being attacked, would certainly alter the tone of the play.

1.1.194–95. but he will wear his cap with suspicion: Fears about husbands being betrayed by their wives and thereby turning into cuckolds are expressed throughout this play, as Gail Kern Paster points out in her "Modern Perspective." The word *cuckold* comes from the name of the cuckoo, a bird which does not build a nest but instead leaves its eggs for other birds to hatch and feed. The association of cuckolds with horns growing from the forehead goes back to ancient times and may originate with the early and prevalent practice of "grafting the spurs of a castrated cock on the root of the excised comb, where they grew and became horns, sometimes of several inches long" (*OED*, "horn" 7a).

1.2.0 SD. brother to Leonato: In the early printed versions of *Much Ado* there is a character, "an old man, brother to Leonato," who is identified in stage directions and speech prefixes throughout the play as "old" or "brother"; in one scene of the play (2.1) there is also a masked character addressed as "Signior Antonio" and identified in speech prefixes as "Antho." Because Leonato calls his brother "Anthony" in 5.1 and because the masked Signior Antonio who dances with Ursula in 2.1 is spoken of by Ursula as if he, like Leonato's brother, were an "old man," with his head "waggling" and his hand "dry," Nicholas Rowe (in 1709) and all editors since have identified Leonato's brother with the Signior Antonio of 2.1 and have thus called the brother "Antonio" in all speech prefixes and stage directions. Unfortunately, this conflation of the brother with Signior Antonio creates a problem in 2.1, where Leonato and his brother (who enters with Leonato at the beginning of the scene) are the hosts of the supper to which Don Pedro and his company are invited. For Leonato's brother to join with the maskers (as "Signior Antonio") and dance with Ursula, he has either to be sent offstage (with, "Brother, give good room") and for some unexplained reason put on a mask and reenter with the masked guests, or (as some current editors would have it) both Leonato and the brother must mask as the masked guests enter. To have Leonato's brother (and Leonato) mask is to break with the convention of masking in other plays of the period—for example, in *Romeo and Juliet* and *Henry VIII*—where the outside revelers come in masked and the unmasked hosts greet them. We do not find the reasons for conflating the brother and "Signior Antonio" persuasive enough to outweigh the awkwardness that occurs when they are conflated; we therefore keep separate the masked Signior Antonio of 2.1 and Leonato's unmasked brother, whom we designate "Leonato's brother" throughout the play.

2.1.83 SD. Drum: The dialogue that appears in lines 84–149 can be imagined as spoken as the couples move forward and aside in an opening stately processional dance, or pavan; such a dance would be accompanied by the tabor and probably one or two other instruments. The **Music for the dance** called for in the Folio (in our text at line 148 SD) and the **Dance** called for in the quarto (in our text at line 152 SD) would likely call for a larger number of musicians as the couples join in a galliard or some other dance appropriate for masked "reveling." It is quite possible, however, that the dialogue in lines 84–149 precedes any dancing, and simply reflects the conversation of the couples as they begin to "pair off" for the dance that begins at line 152.

2.1.98 SP. **Benedick:** The early printed texts give this speech and the two following to Benedick and the remaining two to Balthasar. Most editors assume that the speech prefixes are in error and either give all of the speeches to Balthasar or, because of what happens later in the play, give all of them to Borachio. Given the play's emphasis on Benedick as a womanizer, and given his flirtation with Margaret in 5.1, we have decided to follow the early printed texts in the speech assignments.

2.1.196–98. **now . . . post:** Editors find parallels with a story in *Lazarillo de Tormes* about a boy and his blind master. In this mid-sixteenth-century picaresque novel, the boy steals the blind man's meat and tricks the blind man into knocking himself unconscious on a stone pillar, at one point called a "post." Although there are a few points of similarity, the Lazarillo story does not in any way illustrate the moral of Benedick's statement.

2.1.250. **Hercules:** Hercules was briefly the slave of the queen of Lydia, Omphale, and on surviving Greek vases is pictured as spinning wool for her. Turning the roasting spit would be a more demeaning occupation.

2.2.44. Claudio: Those who substitute "Borachio" for "Claudio" in this speech argue that the plot that Borachio is setting up would require Margaret, in her role as Hero, to call Borachio by his own name; to call him "Claudio," they argue, would suggest to onlookers that she was being deceived by an impostor rather than being unfaithful. Those who follow the early printed text and retain "Claudio" argue that Margaret may be led to think that she and Borachio are pretending to be Hero and Claudio. Since we never learn how Borachio persuades Margaret to take part in the deception, we have no way of knowing if she calls him "Claudio" as part of the game they are playing or whether the text is in error here.

3.3.117–18. the fashion . . . is nothing to a man: Editors have suggested that Borachio here begins leading up to a major point—either that Claudio, in turning against Hero, has been more inconstant than the fickleness of the fashions, or that Hero's clothing has led Claudio to mistake Margaret for Hero. In either case, Borachio's "fashion is nothing to a man"—which might mean "the style of his clothes does not matter to a man" or "clothes do not make the man"—is understood by Conrade to mean *"clothes* are nothing to a man,*"* a statement he rejects by saying that "clothes are apparel."

3.3.172 SD. Enter Dogberry: We agree with J. C. Meagher (*Shakespeare Quarterly,* 1972) and F. H. Mares (The New Cambridge Shakespeare *Much Ado*) that Dogberry should reenter at this point. Dogberry, at line 84, ordered the Watch to summon him if anything important happened, and Seacoal tells a fellow watchman to "Call up the right Master Constable" at line 167. The speeches and speech headings for lines 173–77 are so

garbled in the early printed text that editorial interven-
tion is almost mandatory. Our solution to the textual
problems here is to have Dogberry reenter and to assign
lines 173 and 176–77 to him. In the quarto, the speech
headings for these lines read *Conr;* Mares suggests that
Con., for "Constable," could have been intended. (*Con*
is, in fact, what is printed in the quarto in its earlier [its
so-called "uncorrected"] state.) Despite his own persuasive argument, Mares does not have Dogberry reenter.

4.1.87. Hero itself can blot out Hero's virtue: The
dialogue in lines 82–87—

> HERO
> What kind of catechizing call you this?
> CLAUDIO
> To make you answer truly to your name.
> HERO
> Is it not Hero? Who can blot that name
> With any just reproach?
> CLAUDIO   Marry, that can Hero!
> Hero itself can blot out Hero's virtue—

has suggested to many editors connections with the
Anglican catechism and with the legends about the
lovers named Hero and Leander, made popular through
Christopher Marlowe's poem named for the lovers.
The "Catechism for Children" included in the section
on "Confirmation" in the Anglican Book of Common
Prayer (1559) opens with the question "What is your
name?" (Other Anglican catechisms—such as King
Edward's Catechism of 1553 and *A Briefe and necessary
Catechism or Instruction* of 1575—begin with quite
different questions.) Even though other catechisms did
not ask the child its name, and even though "catechizing" could simply mean "questioning," it is quite possible that the combination of Hero's question about

"catechizing" and Claudio's response about her answering to her name might have echoed, for Shakespeare's original audiences, the opening of the Book of Common Prayer catechism and its emphasis on the connection between naming, baptism, and a Christian life.

The relationship between Hero's name and that of the heroine of Marlowe's *Hero and Leander* is much more problematic. It has been argued that the legendary Hero had come to be seen as an example of female constancy, since she killed herself when her lover, Leander, drowned while swimming the Hellespont to visit her. It is equally likely that the legendary Hero (who was a nun—although, in Marlowe, a nun of Venus) was seen as an example of the way a good Renaissance woman should not behave, since she broke her vows by admitting Leander into her bed. How a Renaissance audience would have responded to the legendary Hero's name would give two possible, opposite readings of line 87. The line could mean: "You, as a wanton woman, put a blot on the virtues of the name of the legendary Hero," or "The very name of the unchaste legendary Hero puts a blot on any virtues you might have."

Textual Notes

The reading of the present text appears to the left of the square bracket. Unless otherwise noted, the reading to the left of the bracket is from **Q**, the First Quarto text (upon which this edition is based). The earliest sources of readings not in Q are indicated as follows: **F** is the First Folio of 1623; **F2** is the Second Folio of 1632; **F3** is the Third Folio of 1663–64; **F4** is the Fourth Folio of 1685; **Ed.** is an earlier editor of Shakespeare, beginning with Rowe in 1709. No sources are given for emendations of punctuation or for corrections of obvious typographical errors, like turned letters that produce no known word. **SD** means stage direction; **SP** means speech prefix; **uncorr.** means the first or uncorrected state of the First Quarto; **corr.** means the second or corrected state of the First Quarto; ~ stands in place of a word already quoted before the square bracket; ʌ indicates the omission of a punctuation mark.

1.1.   0. SD *Messina*] Ed.; *Messina, Innogen his wife* Q

      2, 10. Pedro] Q (Peter)

      15. lion.] ~, Q

      41. bird-bolt] Q (Burbolt)

      58. stuffing—well] ~ ʌ ~ Q

      63. that.] ~, Q

      87. Claudio!] ~, Q

      87. Benedick] Q (Benedict)

      90. Do,] ~ ʌ Q

      94 *and hereafter to 2.1.314.* SP PRINCE] this ed.; *Pedro* Q

      111. SP BENEDICK] Q (*Be.*)

      114–15. talking, . . . Benedick,] Q

141. i'] Q (a)
144. all, Leonato.—] ~: ~, Q
152–53. lord, . . . brother,] ~, . . . ~: Q
154 *and hereafter to 2.2.55.* SP DON JOHN]
    Ed.; *Iohn* Q
199. SD *Pedro*] Ed.; *Pedro, Iohn the bastard* Q
259. vilely] Q (vildly)
261. hire ᵥ] ~: Q
268. hours.] ~, Q
274. you—] ~. Q
276. it—] ~. Q
280. sometimes] Q (sometime)
281. neither.] ~, Q
302. words.] ~, Q

1.2.   0. SD *meeting*] Ed.; *and* Q
    3 *and hereafter in this scene.* SP LEONATO'S
      BROTHER] this ed.; *Old* Q
    27. skill] F; shill Q

1.3.   22–23. root ᵥ . . . yourself.] ~, . . . ~, Q
    38. SD *1 line later in* Q
    47. brother's] F; bothers Q
    52. on] Q (one)
    67. me?] ~. Q
    70. o'] Q (a)

2.1.   0. SD *brother, Hero . . . niece, with . . .*
      Margaret] Ed.; *brother, his wife, Hero*
      . . . niece, and a kinsman. Q
    2 *and hereafter in this scene.* SP LEONATO'S
      BROTHER] *this ed.; brother* Q
    40. bearherd] Q (Berrord)
    42. SP LEONATO] *Lenoato* Q
    66. you.] ~, Q
    72, 74. jig] ijgge Q
    83. SD *Prince ᵥ Pedro . . . and Don John*]
      Ed.; *prince, Pedro . . . or dumb Iohn* Q
    83. SD *with a Drum . . . all in masks*] F
      (Maskers with a drum); not in Q

84. a bout] about Q
86. So$_\wedge$] ~, Q
148. SD F, *4 lines later; not in* Q
192. drover] Q (Drouier)
207. SD *Leonato*] this ed.; *Leonato, Iohn and Borachio, and Conrade.* Q
293–94. father$_\wedge$ . . . obtained.] ~, . . . ~, Q
299. cue] Q (Qu)
307. it, . . . fool,] ~, . . . ~$_\wedge$ Q
325. o'] Q (a)
340. SP PRINCE] this ed.; *Pedro* Q
365. too,] ~$_\wedge$ Q

2.2.   43. Margaret term] Q (Marg terme)
2.3.   7. SD *1 line earlier in* Q
25. an] Q (and)
36. SD *Claudio . . . music*] Ed.; *Claudio, Musicke* Q; "*Enter Balthaser with musicke*" *6 lines later in* Q
64. SP BALTHASAR *sings*] Ed.; *The Song* Q *corr.; The Song* [*g* inverted] Q *uncorr.*
76–79. *so, . . . nonny*] so, &c. Q
87. lief] Q (liue)
94. SD *1 line earlier in* Q
108–9. it, . . . affection,] Q
143. us of] F; of us Q
159. sometimes] Q (sometime)
184–85. well. . . . love,] ~, . . . ~, Q
249. Against] Aganst Q

3.1.   0. SD and 4 *Ursula*] Q (*Ursley*)
9. enter,] ~: Q
63. featured,] ~. Q
67. antic] Q (antique)
69. vilely] Q (vildly)
101. bearing,] ~$_\wedge$ Q
117. on; . . . will] on . . . will Q *corr.;* one . . . wil Q *uncorr.*

3.2.   19–20. love. . . . sad,] ~, . . . ~, Q
           27. can] Ed.; cannot Q
           39. o'] Q (a)
           51. SP PRINCE] F; *Bene.* Q
           65. toothache.—] ~, Q
           73 *and hereafter to 4.1.70.* SP DON JOHN]
                Ed.; *Bastard* Q
           74. e'en] Q (den)
           79. of‸] Q *uncorr.;* ~, Q *corr.*
           90. manifest.] ~, Q
      90–91. brother, I . . . heart‸] Ed.; ~, ~ . . . ~,
                Q *uncorr.;* ~ (~ . . . ~) Q *corr.*
           91. holp] Q *corr.* (holpe); hope Q *uncorr.*
      96–97. for . . . of,] (for . . . talking of) Q *corr.;*
                ‸for . . . talking, Q *uncorr.*
         105. me‸] Q *corr.;* ~, Q *uncorr.*
         107. her‸ then,] ~, ~ ‸ Q
         117. her,] ~ ‸ Q
         117. congregation,] Q *corr.;* ~ ‸ Q *uncorr.*
3.3.   15. name.] ~, Q *uncorr.;* ~: Q *corr.*
      17, 27. SP SEACOAL] Ed.; *Watch 2* Q
         17. constable—] ~. Q
         24. lantern] Q (lanthorne)
      37, 66. SP SECOND WATCHMAN] this ed.; *Watch*
                Q
   44, 48, 53. SP SEACOAL] this ed.; *Watch* Q
  87, 95, 105. SP SEACOAL] Ed.; *Watch* Q
       107. Don] F; Dun Q
       123. deformed] Q *corr.;* defermed Q *uncorr.*
       125. SP FIRST WATCHMAN] this ed.; *Watch* Q
   126–27. year. He . . . down] yeere, a . . . downe
                Q *corr.;* yeere‸ a . . . down Q *uncorr.*
       127. I] Q *corr.; omit* Q *uncorr.*
       134. reechy] Q (rechie)
   134, 135. sometimes] Q (sometime)
       148. vilely] Q (vildly)

149–50. Prince, . . . planted˄] ~ ˄ . . . ~. Q
153. SP CONRADE] *Conr.* Q *corr.; Con.* Q
   uncorr.
154. SP BORACHIO] *Bar.* Q
156. oaths,] ~. Q
167. SP SEACOAL] this ed.; *Watch* 2 Q
173, 176. SP DOGBERRY] this ed. (*after J. C. Mea-*
   gher, "Conrade Conned: or, the career
   of Hugh Oatcake," Shakespeare Quarterly *24 (1972): 90–92; Conr* Q *corr.;*
   Con. or *Con* Q *uncorr.*
173. masters—] ~. Q
174. SP FIRST WATCHMAN] Ed.; *Watch* 2 Q
177. speak, . . . you,] Q
180. SP CONRADE] *Conr.* Q *corr.; Con.* Q
   uncorr.

3.4.   1. Good] Q *corr.;* God Q *uncorr.*
18. in] F; it Q
19, 43, 45. o'] Q (a)

3.5.   0. SD *Leonato, and*] Q *uncorr.; Leonati,*
   and Q *corr.*
2, 6, 9, 15, 18, 23, 32, 41, 43. SP DOGBER-
   RY] Ed.; *Const. Dog.* Q
7, 13, 27, 29. SP VERGES] Ed.; *Headb.* Q
9. off] Q (of)
23. an] and't Q
32. talking.] ~ ˄ Q
34. see!—] ~, Q *uncorr.;* ~: Q *corr.*
37. troth he is, as] Q *corr.;* ~, ~ ~ ˄ ~ Q
   uncorr.
50. SP DOGBERRY] Ed.; *Constable* Q
54. SD *4 lines earlier in* Q

4.1.   4. SP FRIAR] *Fran.* Q
26. SP LEONATO] *Leonata* Q
29. SP PRINCE] *Princn* Q
48. virginity—] ~. Q

57. thee,] ~ ˄ Q
91. SP HERO] Q *corr. (Hero); Bero* Q *uncorr.*
100. SP DON JOHN] Ed.; *Iohn* Q
116. SP DON JOHN] Ed.; *Bastard* Q
120. Benedick!] ~, Q *corr.;* ~ ˄ Q *uncorr.*
126. up?] Q *corr.* (vp?); ~. Q *uncorr.*
128. Why,] ~ ˄ Q
131. eyes,] Q *uncorr.* (eies,); ~: Q *corr.*
145. on,] ~ ˄ Q
146–47. mine, . . . her—] ~: . . . ~, Q
156. Lady,] Q *corr.;* ~ ˄ Q *uncorr.*
165. silent been] Ed.; bin silent Q
166–67. fortune, . . . lady.] ~, . . . ~, Q
176. tenor] Q (tenure)
200–1. not. . . . her.] ~, . . . ~, Q
213. princes . . . dead.] Q *as* "princesse (left for dead,)"
228. out˄] ~. Q
239. moving,] ~ ˄ Q
307. here.] ~, Q
318. hand˄] ~: Q
309, 322, 325. Beatrice—] ~. Q
328. Beat—] ~? Q

4.2.
0. SD *Enter . . . Borachio*] Ed.; *Enter the Constables, Borachio, and the Towne clearke in gownes.* Q
1. SP DOGBERRY] Ed.; *Keeper* Q
2, 5, 70. SP VERGES] Ed.; *Cowley* Q
4. SP DOGBERRY] Ed.; *Andrew* Q
7. offenders˄] ~? Q
10, 13, 17, 20, 27, 32, 38, 43, 46, 52, 58, 72, 76. SP DOGBERRY] Ed.; *Kemp* Q
19. SP BORACHIO/CONRADE] Q (*Both*)
45. constable—] ~. Q
49. SP SEACOAL] this ed.; *Watch 2* Q
53. SP VERGES] *Const.* Q

61. SP SEACOAL] this ed.; *Watch* Q
69. SP DOGBERRY] *Constable* Q
70–71. hands— | CONRADE Off, coxcomb!] Ed.;
     hands of Coxcombe Q
74. them.—] ~, Q
75. SP CONRADE] Ed.; *Couley* Q

5.1.   1 *and hereafter throughout this scene.* SP
     LEONATO'S BROTHER] this ed.; *Brother*
     Q
17. Bid] Ed.; And Q
48. e'en . . . e'en] Q (den . . . den)
50. lords—] ~? Q
97. Brother—] ~. Q
103, 112. Anthony—] ~. Q
108. anticly] Q (antiquely)
109. off] Q (of)
119. lord—] ~. Q
121. No?] ~ ͜ Q
122. SD *Leonato . . . exit.*] this ed.; *Exeunt*
     amb. Q, *1 line earlier*
128. like] F2; likt Q
130. brother.] ~ ͜ Q
141. wit.] ~, Q
149. me.] ~, Q
161. sweet] sweeete Q
167. him.] ~ ͜ Q
169. naught.] ~, Q
194. on] Q (one)
204. Lackbeard ͜ there,] ~, ~ ͜ Q
215. up,] ~ ͜ Q
216. SD *4 lines earlier in* Q
217, 225, 264, 319, 330, 333, 336. SP DOG-
     BERRY] Ed.; *Const.* Q
268. SP VERGES] Ed.; *Con. 2* Q
278–79. men— . . . fled—] ~, . . . ~ ͜ Q

5.2.   9. me? Why,] ~, ~ ͜ Q

          25. SD *1 line earlier in* Q

          29. *deserve*—] ~. Q

          41. SD *2 lines later in* Q

          68. think.] ~, Q

          86. myself.] ~ ^ Q

5.3.   3. *slanderous*] slauderous Q

         10. dumb] F (dombe); dead Q

         11. SP Now] Ed.; *Claudio* Now Q

         17. *groan* ^] ~. Q

         22. SP CLAUDIO] Ed.; *Lo.* Q

         32. speed 's] Q (speeds)

5.4.   0. SD *Leonato's brother*] this ed.; *old man*

               Q

         5. will, . . . appears ^] ~ ^ . . . ~, Q

         7 *and hereafter.* SP LEONATO'S BROTHER]

            this ed.; *Old* Q

         41. Benedick] Q (Bened.)

         53. SD *1 line earlier in* Q

     69–70. qualify, . . . ended,] Q

         82. cousin,] ~ ^ Q

     102. SP BENEDICK] Ed.; *Leon.* Q

     102. Peace!] ~ ^ Q

     125. play,] ~ ^ Q

Much Ado About Nothing:
A Modern Perspective
Gail Kern Paster

Cuckoldry jokes are in the air in Messina. Its governor, Leonato, snatches one out of it when he jokes feebly about having to ask his wife repeatedly for reassurance as to his daughter's legitimacy:

PRINCE I think this is your daughter.
LEONATO Her mother hath *many times* told me so.[1]
(1.1.102–3)

Benedick draws our attention to this trace of an old suspicion: "Were you in doubt, sir, that you asked her?" (1.1.104). But Benedick, we soon learn, is also suspicious of women as the agents of men's humiliation and defeat. He expresses an almost pathological fear of betrayal in marriage: to be married is to wear the conventional horns of a cuckold, to have one's own military bugle snatched away, to have it sounded in one's own face:

> That a woman conceived me, I thank her; that she brought me up, I likewise give her most humble thanks. But that I will have a recheat winded [i.e., a bugle-call blown] in my forehead or hang my bugle in an invisible baldrick, all women shall pardon me. Because I will not do them the wrong to mistrust any, I will do myself the right to trust none.
> (1.1.234–40)

213

Benedick's extraordinary self-portrait of his relations with women yields readily to a psychoanalytic reading. Moving without pause from his conception to his upbringing to his cuckolding, he conflates his relations to mother and to wife, collapses past and future, memories and fears.[2] What seems to unify all these stages of a man's life, for Benedick, is humiliating dependence on women, beginning with the infant's dependence on maternal women for life and nurture. But that early dependence, instead of being outgrown, is seen here as forerunner to the later sexual humiliations of the adult male. Furthermore, Benedick's dismissive mention of his mother as the "woman [who] conceived me" betrays her real importance to the structure of repressed memory. In psychoanalytic narratives of male repression, the mother's lack of the phallus is a disturbing image for the child—an image of his own fear of castration and of his overmastering by another male. But for Benedick, the returning soldier, this fear of women seems less generic than personal: the cuckold's horns that he envisions as his own future headdress are specifically those of a defeated soldier who has lost his bugle to another soldier. It is not surprising, then, that Benedick's anticipation of a farewell to arms here parallels Othello's lament for the loss of heroic identity through an imagined sexual betrayal by Desdemona:

> Farewell the tranquil mind! Farewell content!
> Farewell the plumèd troops and the big wars
> That makes ambition virtue! O, farewell!
> Farewell the neighing steed and the shrill trump,
> The spirit-stirring drum, th' ear-piercing fife,
> The royal banner, and all quality,
> Pride, pomp, and circumstance of glorious war!
>   (*Othello* 3.3.400–6)

Musicians with drums and fife. (2.3.14)
From Thomas Lant, *Sequitur celebritas & pompa funeris . . .* (1587).

For soldiers like Benedick and Othello, marriage threat-
ens loss of a valued form of masculine singleness, a loss
of control.

More interesting, perhaps, in a comic action like
Much Ado's which is organized around the imagining of
sexual betrayal, is that the fear of being associated with
the cuckold's horns is not peculiar to men nor is
resistance to marriage a symptom of only masculine
identity. Though her uncles worry that Beatrice's sharp
tongue makes her "too curst" (2.1.20) to get a husband,
she jokes that she will thereby avoid making her husband wear horns: "I shall lessen God's sending that way,
for it is said 'God sends a curst cow short horns,' but to a
cow too curst, he sends none" (2.1.21–24). Even the
devil, no mere mortal, wears the signs of betrayal;
Beatrice imagines having him meet her looking "like an
old cuckold with horns on his head" (2.1.44–45). The
horn motif continues to sound in the play even after it
ostensibly has been silenced by the exposure of Don
John's sexual slander against Hero. Thus Benedick,
though converted to love in the person of Beatrice,
nonetheless misogynistically urges the play's remaining
eligible bachelor, Don Pedro, to join in the march to the
altar in the spirit of accepting a universal, age-old
humiliation: "Get thee a wife, get thee a wife. There is no
staff more reverend than one tipped with horn" (5.4.126–
28). If betrayal is the universal fate of the married, it is
no wonder that Beatrice regards marriage as a form of
repentance:

> . . . wooing, wedding, and repenting is as a Scotch
> jig, a measure, and a cinquepace. The first suit is
> hot and hasty like a Scotch jig, and full as fantasti-
> cal; the wedding, mannerly modest as a measure,
> full of state and ancientry; and then comes repen-

tance, and with his bad legs falls into the cinquepace faster and faster till he sink into his grave.
(2.1.72–78)[3]

As all these quotations suggest, anxiety about sexual
betrayal in marriage seems endemic in Messina, sparing
neither the old nor the young, neither male nor female.
What is clear in the men's cuckoldry jokes is their willful
silence, for the sake of male friendship and preservation
of the status quo, about the male betrayer and a contrasting emphasis on his female partner. It is not the desires
of other men that Benedick mistrusts but those of
womenkind. It is only when they are among themselves
that the Men's Club of Messina—to borrow Harry
Berger's wonderful appellation—allows Balthasar's
song to register an alternative truth: "Sigh no more,
ladies, sigh no more, / Men were deceivers ever, / One
foot in sea and one on shore, / To one thing constant
never" (2.3.64–67).[4]

Much Ado is not unusual in its reiterated wordplay on
horns, since jokes about the wearing of cuckolds' horns
are commonplace throughout the literature of this
period. But, in the drama of the period, there is a
marked disparity between the frequency of the jokes and
the infrequency of wifely infidelity. Many more wives
are falsely accused than are, in fact, guilty. This dis-
crepancy between fears of betrayal and actual guilt
suggests that we should focus less on the infidelity itself
than on the real source of patriarchal anxiety, which
was patriarchy's inevitable dependence on (and inability
to verify) the chastity of wives and mothers. For only
such chastity secured a social structure based on legiti-
mate inheritance of lands, wealth, property, rank, and
name.

In *Much Ado*, I want to suggest, this patriarchal

anxiety gives cuckoldry jokes a particular, local function. They work to resolve a social contradiction in
Elizabethan society, a moment of double bind in the
cultural history of marriage in which an authoritarian
official tradition collided with an emergent ideal. Sixteenth-century English society had not yet dispensed
with forms of overt, virulent misogyny inherited from
medieval Catholicism which made marriage, especially
for men, a less perfect way of life than celibacy. But it
could not readily accommodate these inherited forms of
misogyny to a post-Reformation celebration of marriage, particularly in its modern form of companionate,
consensual unions in which the emotional satisfaction
of both partners assumes new importance. Elizabethan
society could not dispense with misogyny because the
most general, even ancient function of antifeminist
discourse is to justify patriarchy's unequal distribution
of power and property, its subordination of women. But
virulent suspicion of wifely chastity—the kind of suspicion that destroys lives and marriages in *Othello* and
The Winter's Tale, for example—must have seemed
incompatible with an emergent theory of marriage
focused upon the initial consent of both partners and
upon their long-term fulfillment of a set of mutual
obligations which were in part material, in part emotional.[5] Even Don Pedro, in seeking to promote the
marriage of Hero and Claudio, assumes that winning
the consent of Hero comes before anything else: "I
will break *with her* and with her father" (1.1.304), while
Beatrice slyly urges her cousin not to say "Father, as
it please you" but rather "Father, as it please me"
(2.1.53, 55–56). If women's feelings matter, then so, it
would seem, do feelings about women: medieval misogyny and post-Reformation marriage theory could
not comfortably coexist. From the tension between

them, the double plots of Shakespeare's comedy come into being.

Perhaps such a reading of *Much Ado* seems obvious. Any reader of the play can see how much of its action is devoted to overcoming, through Don Pedro's theatrical manipulations, the resistance to love expressed by both Beatrice and Benedick. But to follow this reading to its logical conclusion will require the replacement of a character-based interpretation of the play with one which dissolves boundaries between the text as an autonomous work of art and the culture in which it is produced. Such a reading will attend to the widely dispersed misogyny in Elizabethan culture which speaks in and through Benedick, and to the effects of that misogyny as they register in Beatrice's resistance. Thus, where I depart from traditional critics is in refusing to accept Beatrice and Benedick's resistance to marriage as finally psychological in significance, even if it is expressed in psychological form in their language and behavior. I do not wish to explain resistance to marriage as idiosyncratic aspects of the personalities of Beatrice and Benedick, even though such resistance is what most sets them apart from their friends and kinfolk. Nor do I wish to interpret their eventual declarations of mutual affection as the manifestation of a hidden attraction that was there all along. I take their love as the creation of Don Pedro, who would "fain have it a match," he says, to enliven the time between Claudio's betrothal and nuptials by accomplishing a difficult thing. And presumably he also wishes to make sure that no person in his lordly jurisdiction escapes from the paradoxical cultural requirement to pair off *freely.*

But the uncomfortable truth is that, in a misogynistic culture, resistance to marriage is rational, not idiosyncratic, because misogyny—defined as the systematic denigration of women—gives men and women well-founded reasons to suspect one another. Beatrice and Benedick are given the function in this play of wittily enacting for our benefit the conventional postures of mutual antagonism so that their eventual union will seem both to ratify the irrational force of desire (no matter how it is brought into being) and to dissolve the larger social tensions exemplified by their mutual mistrust. Because, even though marriage might appear incompatible with individual peace of mind, it remains the basic form of social organization, the central distribution point in Elizabethan society for the social and sexual goods of adult maturity. This paradox about marriage may serve to explain why Don Pedro, rather than take a laissez-faire position with regard to the wooing and resistance to wooing in his midst, intervenes personally as head of the social order in the double matchmakings of Hero to Claudio, Beatrice to Benedick. Indeed, he has a notable, almost quantifying pragmatism with regard to affection, assuaging Claudio's fear that his "liking might too sudden seem" with a breezy "What need the bridge much broader than the flood? / The fairest grant is the necessity. / Look what will serve is fit" (1.1.311–13).

It is important for my argument to emphasize that the history of misogyny is also the history of romantic love, that cultivation of antifeminist feeling has, since the early twelfth century in Europe, coexisted with, indeed depended upon, a counterbalancing idealization of woman. As Howard Bloch has argued, "Misogyny and courtly love are coconspiring abstractions of the feminine whose function was from the start, and continues to be, the diversion of women from history by the annihilation of the identity of individual women . . . and

Matrimonium :

The marriage yoke. (1.1.197)
From Henry Peacham, *Minerua Britanna* . . . (1612).

thus the transformation of woman into an ideal."[6] That
is to say, the idealism of romantic love and the denigration of antifeminist rhetoric are alike in functioning to
erase differences between women in order to make
women anonymous and invisible to historical action.
Such an erasure of differences in women is precisely
what occurs in Benedick's lines quoted above, where
the distinct roles of mother and wife are subsumed
into the one undifferentiated category, Woman. In the
logic of misogyny, if one woman is treacherous, all
women are condemned: "Because I will not do them
the wrong to mistrust any, I will do myself the right to
trust none." The point is not only, as Harry Berger has
argued, that "the difference between men and women
in this respect . . . is that women are responsible for
their sins but men are not."[7] Even more crucial is to
recognize the instability between a misogyny which
posits all Women-as-the-Same and an idealization
which posits Women-as-Different.[8] In the conversations
between Claudio and Benedick—as in the similar
conversations between Romeo and Mercutio—this
instability in the categorization of women is easy to
detect: "Can the world buy such a jewel" as Hero, ideal-
ist Claudio asks rhetorically. "Yea," comes the misogynist's bawdy reply, "and a case [vagina] to put it into"
(1.1.177–78).

Indeed, this instability in the way women are catego-
rized would seem to motivate the different rhetorics by
which Benedick and Beatrice are each persuaded to
love. While Benedick must be led to believe in Beatrice
as Different from all other women, Beatrice must be
brought to accept herself as just the Same. Hence
Benedick is made to overhear a conversation among the
men which describes Beatrice as a compendium of
virtues—"an excellent sweet lady," "out of all suspicion

A pleached bower. (1.2.9–10, 3.1.7–9)
From T[homas] F[ella],
A book of diverse devices . . . (1585–98, 1622).

. . . virtuous," "exceeding wise" (2.3.166–68)—except for her dotage on Benedick. Beatrice, by contrast, learns from Hero and Ursula less about Benedick's virtues than about her own faults, the chief of which is the nonconformity of resistance: "to be so odd and from all fashions / As Beatrice is cannot be commendable" (3.1.76–77). Both resisters are asked to understand the other's alleged passion as unwilled and uncontrollable —the real thing, in other words. Beatrice and Benedick experience their separate reactions to this surprising news as free and fortuitous. Benedick, on cue, vows to "be horribly in love with her" (2.3.237). Beatrice, stung by what she has overheard, thereupon commits herself to a course of action she names self-taming, "taming my wild heart to thy loving hand" (3.1.118). But we have heard Don Pedro gloat, "The sport will be when they hold one an opinion of another's dotage, and no such matter" (2.3.218–20), and we thus have reason to think otherwise about the relative freedom of their actions. We witness the conspirators glorying in the emotional transformations which, in the guise of "love gods" (2.1.377), they claim to have achieved; and we note in their language a deterministic vocabulary of contagion and entrapment. Claudio whispers to the Prince that Benedick has "ta'en th' infection" (2.3.129); Hero and Ursula congratulate themselves on having "limed," or trapped, Beatrice (3.1.309). Thus in the contrast between Beatrice and Benedick's subjective experience of free choice in love and the undeniable presence of social manipulation in bringing them to imagine that freedom, we can recognize the powerful, because invisible, workings of ideological conditioning to make people act, so they think, naturally: "the world," as Benedick grandiosely declares, "must be peopled" (2.3.244–45).

But since early modern English patriarchy required both marriage and misogyny, the social inscription that works so hard to create romantic love works equally hard to destabilize it. Thematic links between the two institutions of marriage and misogyny are emphasized because, in the double plot of *Much Ado About Nothing*, the actions to make and to break nuptials employ the same kinds of theatrical means. Shakespeare assigns the function of destroyer with evident symmetry to Don Pedro's brother, Don John the Bastard, whose sense of self-expression in trying to abort the nuptials of Claudio and Hero matches Don Pedro's in bringing them about. If the moral differences between the two brothers seem too insistently coded, that may be—as Jean Howard has argued—because the play is ambivalent about the social and moral function of theatrical practice.[9] By making the Iago-like Don John a bastard who is so determined to avenge his defeat at the hands of Claudio that he does not scruple to scapegoat Hero in the process, Shakespeare defines one kind of theatrical manipulation as evil, that is, as motivated by the urge to destroy. But is the moral character of Don Pedro's delight in theatrical practices thereby enhanced? The answer to that question cannot be unproblematical, given that Don Pedro's surrogate wooing of Hero leads to a series of early misapprehensions—that the Prince woos for himself; that Hero or her father might have preferred to accept the Prince's suit; that love of women breeds mistrust between male friends because, as Claudio says, "beauty is a witch / Against whose charms faith melteth into blood [i.e. sensual appetite]" (2.1.177–78). Nor does Don Pedro's devotion to theatrical practice give him any advantage in seeing through his brother's deception: when the Prince and Claudio witness the scene at Hero's chamber window in which Margaret allows herself to be courted as Hero in Hero's clothes, they see and hear only what Don John has prepared them to: "Go but with me tonight, you shall see her chamber window entered, even the night before her wedding day" (3.2.105–7). The potential moral hollowness and material harm of theatrical practices are later emblematized, in this play, when Claudio stands before what we know to be an empty tomb to read an epitaph for Hero.

The play takes pains to construct Claudio as inexperienced and to emphasize the superficiality of a love which arises, he says, at a moment of postcombat mental vacancy:

> . . . now I am returned and that war thoughts
> Have left their places vacant, in their rooms
> Come thronging soft and delicate desires,
> All prompting me how fair young Hero is,
> Saying I liked her ere I went to wars.
> (1.1.296–300)

The prolongation of courtship—which seems the goal of Shakespeare's other conventional lovers such as Orlando in *As You Like It*, or even Romeo—holds no attraction for the two-dimensional Claudio, nor does Hero use the courtship period as Rosalind does in *As You Like It* to investigate the quality of her lover's desire and imagination. The too-compliant Hero accepts the marriage proposal of a man in a mask and then learns to transfer her consent from the wearer of that mask, Don Pedro, to his young favorite. Claudio does not even plan to spend much time getting acquainted with Hero after their marriage and has to be told that his astonishing plan to accompany Don Pedro home to Aragon would be a great "soil in the new gloss of your marriage" (3.2.5–6). (Indeed, the lovers' activity of courtship as mutual interrogation is taken over in this play by Beatrice and Benedick. Even though this delight in mutual interrogation is one reason why we are conditioned to expect their eventual union, it is also the case that Beatrice and Benedick use the resulting information to bolster resistance to marriage and to improve their jests at each other's expense.) Shakespeare uses Claudio's passivity and inexperience as a wooer to rationalize the young count's readiness to believe Don John's slander of Hero and to prepare us eventually to forgive the misogynistic brutality with which he shames her before the assembled wedding guests:

> O, what authority and show of truth
> Can cunning sin cover itself withal!
> Comes not that blood as modest evidence
> To witness simple virtue? Would you not swear,
> All you that see her, that she were a maid,
> By these exterior shows? But she is none.
> (4.1.35–40)

Claudio's willed commitment to reading Hero's blush as "guiltiness, not modesty" (42) suggests that the real problem linking the two plots of the play is the collapse of the tension between women-as-different and women-as-the-same into one incoherent category of woman-as-different-from-herself. The audience then and the audience now are in a position to understand that widespread cultural suspicion of women, surrogate wooing, and Don John's theatrical illusionism have combined to interrupt the wedding of Hero and Claudio. The audience is also in a position to appreciate the

irony of Benedick and Beatrice relinquishing their resistance to marriage and exchanging protestations of
love at the very moment when the grounds for mutual
suspicion between the sexes seem to have widened. A
subtler irony may reside in the complexities of Benedick's situation as the lapsed misogynist learns of one
danger in love he had not foreseen, one other rational
reason to remain resistant. That is, even as he gives up
misogyny and trusts Beatrice's word for Hero's innocence, he finds a new way in which love may be hazard-
ous to one's health: when he rashly asks Beatrice to
"bid me do anything for thee," she promptly replies,
"Kill Claudio" (4.1.302–3). "Ha! Not for the wide
world," comes his automatic reply.

The recuperative necessities of comic closure that will
not allow Hero to die or remain dishonored by an
unforgiven Claudio also prevent Benedick from having
to follow up on the challenge he flings at Claudio and
Don Pedro, from having to act irrevocably upon his
decision to sacrifice old loyalties to male companions to
new loyalties to his future companion in marriage. But
the final entrance of the bridal party, with not just the
reborn Hero but all the women wearing masks, suggests
that the old cultural categories that produce suspicion and slander remain largely untouched by the theatrical manipulations of the Friar and the rapproche-
ment of Beatrice and Benedick. Even the words of
Claudio's question, "Which is the lady I *must seize*
upon?" (5.4.54) in their traditional suggestions of co-
ercion and violence suggest the social manipulations
that are required to separate men and women from
the companionship of their own sex and precipitate
them into the terrifying private world of heterosexual
union for life. Perhaps this is why Benedick insists on
ending the play not with a wedding but with the state-

ly, regulated movements of a communal dance in which the couples move not singly, but together, and no man is yet wearing horns.

---

1. My emphasis. Note here that the original stage directions include the entrance of Leonato's wife, Innogen, but that editors in this text like others omit her on the plausible ground that she has no words at all, appearing in the text no place but here and in the entrance direction for 2.1. This essay is much indebted to the essays by Carol Cook, Jean E. Howard, and Claire McEachern, which are cited in full in the suggestions for further reading.

2. See Carol Cook, " 'The Sign and Semblance of Her Honor': Reading Gender Difference in *Much Ado About Nothing,*" *PMLA* 101 (1986): 187.

3. For a brilliant application of this speech, see Harry Berger, Jr., "Against the Sink-a-Pace: Sexual and Family Politics in *Much Ado About Nothing,*" *Shakespeare Quarterly* 33 (1982): 302–3.

4. Ibid., p. 308.

5. See Ralph A. Houlbrooke, *English Family Life, 1576–1716* (Oxford: Basil Blackwell, 1988), pp. 15–17. For an extended discussion of seventeenth-century discussions of marriage conduct books, see Mary Beth Rose, *The Expense of Spirit: Love and Sexuality in English Renaissance Drama* (Ithaca: Cornell University Press, 1988), pp. 116–31.

6. Howard Bloch, *Medieval Misogyny and the Invention of Western Romantic Love* (Chicago: University of Chicago Press, 1991), pp. 196–97.

7. Berger, "Against the Sink-a-Pace," p. 307.

8. On this categorical instability, see Peter Stallybrass, "Patriarchal Territories: The Body Enclosed," in *Rewrit-*

ing the Renaissance: The Discourses of Sexual Difference in Early Modern Europe, ed. Margaret W. Ferguson, Maureen Quilligan, and Nancy Vickers (Chicago: University of Chicago Press, 1986), p. 133.

9. Jean E. Howard, "Renaissance antitheatricality and the politics of gender and rank in *Much Ado About Nothing,*" in Jean E. Howard and Marion F. O'Connor, eds., *Shakespeare Reproduced* (London: Methuen, 1987), pp. 172–73.

Further Reading

Much Ado About Nothing

Berger, Harry, Jr. "Against the Sink-a-Pace: Sexual and Family Politics in *Much Ado About Nothing.*" *Shakespeare Quarterly* 33 (1982): 302–13.

Berger writes of *Much Ado*'s Hero, its men, and male solidarity. He examines "the premises of power, cost-avoidance, and fear of love and women" in what he calls "the Men's Club of Messina."

Branagh, Kenneth. *Much Ado About Nothing.* Samuel Goldwyn Co., 1993.

Branagh's popular film features the director as Benedick with Emma Thompson opposite him as Beatrice. Denzel Washington's Don Pedro, Keanu Reeves's Don John, and Michael Keaton's Dogberry support the principals in this lavish treatment, set in a sun-drenched Italian villa.

Cook, Carol. " 'The Sign and Semblance of Her Honor': Reading Gender Difference in *Much Ado About Nothing.*" *Publications of the Modern Language Association of America* 101 (1986): 186–202.

Cook begins by focusing on the play's cuckold jokes as a signal of profound anxiety in both the male characters and in Beatrice, all of whom Cook reads as desiring phallic power. In contrast, the identity of the usually silent Hero is written and rewritten in the male interest. She is first a Diana figure, then a Venus figure, and, at the end when she is "resurrected," again a Diana figure. But, according to Cook the end is problematic: "Hero remains dead in her resurrection, as she is reappropriated to the mode of perception that killed her."

Dawson, Anthony B. "Much Ado About Signifying." *Studies in English Literature* 22 (1982): 211–22.

For Dawson, *Much Ado* subjects to comic scrutiny the art of message-sending itself, as well as the subsequent art of interpretation or, more often, misinterpretation. In view of the indirect and mediated interplay through which the other characters relate to each other, the dangerous appeal to them of Don John is that he offers certainty.

Drakakis, John. "Trust and Transgression: The Discursive Practices of *Much Ado About Nothing*." In *Poststructuralist Readings of English Poetry*, ed. Richard Machin and Christopher Norris. Cambridge: Cambridge University Press, 1987.

To the list of binary oppositions explored in *Ado*, Drakakis adds "trust and transgression." Drakakis argues that the terms are derived differentially and thus "must be defined not positively, in terms of their content, but negatively, by contrast with other items in the same system." The Platonic ideas of unity and harmony based upon "trust" are defined only in terms of their opposite, "transgression," whose author is Don John, and whose image is variously the cuckold, the whore, and the bastard.

Evans, Bertrand. *"Much Ado About Nothing."* In *Shakespeare's Comedies*, pp. 66–87. Oxford: Clarendon Press, 1960.

In his study of what he calls "discrepant awareness" —i.e., differing levels of "who knows what" at any given moment in a play—Evans establishes that the viewer of *Much Ado* holds an advantage over at least some participants during fourteen of the play's seventeen scenes. Exploring the eight "practices" that impel the action, Evans focuses initially on Don John's first "practice" on Claudio—one which, while averted, proves illustrative of a world in which later misunderstandings are possible. For Evans, that later misunderstanding throws especially harsh light upon Claudio, whose callousness throws into relief the "humane and noble sympathy" of Beatrice and Benedick's love.

Garner, Shirley Nelson. "Male Bonding and the Myth of Women's Deception in Shakespeare's Plays." In *Shakespeare's Personality*, ed. Norman Holland, Sidney Homan, and Bernard J. Paris, pp. 135–50. Berkeley: University of California Press, 1989.

Garner argues that the pattern of a male character's reaction to his beloved's actual or imagined infidelity defines and satisfies male psychic needs (such as pent-up misogyny, or fear of women). The pattern eventually allows for his return, actually or imaginatively, to an exclusively male community.

Howard, Jean E. "Renaissance antitheatricality and the politics of gender and rank in *Much Ado About Nothing*." In *Shakespeare Reproduced: The text in history and ideology*, ed. Jean E. Howard and Marion F. O'Connor, pp. 163–87. London: Methuen, 1987.

Howard examines *Much Ado* against a body of anti-theatrical Elizabethan texts concerned with the "nature, control, and morality of theatrical power." While one might expect *Much Ado* to be unequivocally positive in regard to theatricality, the play disciplines those who illegitimately aspire to control theatricality and ultimately returns control to the "better sort." Howard pursues the ideological implications of a text that both limits theatricality and—in its material production—gives it untrammeled expression.

Leggatt, Alexander. *"Much Ado About Nothing."* In *Shakespeare's Comedy of Love.* London: Methuen, 1974. Leggatt places *Much Ado* against other Shakespearean comedies and finds it an experimental attempt at retaining the range and fluidity of *Merchant of Venice* while producing the "harmony of disparate elements" that distinguishes *A Midsummer Night's Dream.* Forgoing thematic analysis for a more directly theatrical approach, Leggatt discovers a complex interplay of formality and naturalism that complicates placing the pure convention of the Claudio-Hero plot against the easy naturalism of Beatrice-Benedick. Ultimately, *Ado* asserts "the idea of human reality at the heart of convention."

Machiavelli, Niccolò. *The Prince* (1513), ed. Robert M. Adams, 2nd ed. New York: Norton, 1992.
Machiavelli, a former member of the Florentine government, offers many detailed narratives of political life in the sixteenth-century Italy that is the setting of *Much Ado About Nothing.*

McEachern, Claire. "Fathering Herself: A Source Study of Shakespeare's Feminism." *Shakespeare Quarterly* 39 (1988): 269–90.
McEachern explores Shakespeare's treatment of sources "less as a transference of ingredients, with sources as sites of mere borrowings, than as a culturally determined reading." Sources, then, are not simply stores of narrative material but contexts that Shakespeare found provocative, "or not provocative enough." Through this approach, McEachern investigates Renaissance patriarchy through a study of fathers and daugh-

ters, using both Shakespeare's literary fathers and those fathers and daughters he presents in his plays.

Neely, Carol Thomas. "Broken Nuptials in Shakespeare's Comedies: *Much Ado About Nothing.*" In *Broken Nuptials in Shakespeare's Plays,* pp. 24–57. New Haven: Yale University Press, 1985.

After surveying Shakespeare's comedies from a feminist perspective with its emphasis on power in courtship, this essay locates *Much Ado* at the "center of the comedies." The play, in Neely's analysis, looks backward to the so-called festive comedies like *A Midsummer Night's Dream* and forward to the complex ethical issues of the so-called problem comedies like *Measure for Measure.*

Osborne, Laurie E. "Dramatic Play in *Much Ado About Nothing:* Wedding the Italian Novella and English Comedy." *Philological Quarterly* 69 (1990): 167–88.

Pursuing Shakespeare's reworking of the Italian novellas that are *Much Ado*'s source, Osborne suggests that Shakespeare's principal interest lies in the powers of dramatic play: "staging scenes, acting roles, and creating spectacles." In linking the two principal players—Don Pedro and Don John—Shakespeare reveals the difficulties of absorbing the noncomic, nondramatic materials of his source into comic conventions. For Osborne, the process of creating comedy from noncomic sources requires the manufacture of disasters and oppositions, a process that reveals contradictions at the heart of comedy.

Prouty, Charles Tyler. *The Sources of "Much Ado About Nothing."* New Haven: Yale University Press, 1950.

Prouty's emphasis is "upon the structure, characters, and thematic unity of the play rather than the background." Thus Prouty records and interprets Shakespeare's alterations to the Hero-Claudio plot as received from the sources. Prouty then shows how Shakespeare, having reduced the role of Hero and having recast Claudio, required a comic counterpart—the story of Beatrice and Benedick, apparently Shakespeare's invention.

Roberts, Jeanne Addison. "Strategies of Delay in Shakespeare: What the *Much Ado* is Really About." *Renaissance Papers 1987* (1988), pp. 98–102.
Roberts explores techniques used to delay lovers' unions in the comedies and romances. She discusses in particular how Benedick is restored to his full faculties before his marriage.

Rossiter, A. P. "*Much Ado About Nothing*." In *Angels with Horns*, pp. 67–81. London: Longmans, Green, 1961. Reprinted in *Shakespeare, The Comedies: A Collection of Critical Essays*, ed. Kenneth Muir, pp. 47–57. Englewood Cliffs, N.J.: Prentice-Hall, 1965.
Rossiter distinguishes the sorts of humor in *Much Ado About Nothing*, tracing all to a cumulative effect of "impetuous exuberance," a tone most manifest in quick and competitive manipulation of language. Yet Rossiter points out that equivocations are restricted to appearance and do not extend into ambivalence toward things themselves (love, for example). This quality leads Rossiter to place *Much Ado* within Shakespeare's canon "just at the point" before the equilibrium between jest and fortune ("where fortune favors the laughers") turns to cynicism.

Shakespeare's Language

Abbott, E. A. *A Shakespearian Grammar.* New York: Haskell House, 1972.

This compact reference book, first published in 1870, helps with many difficulties in Shakespeare's language. It systematically accounts for a host of differences between Shakespeare's usage and sentence structure and our own.

Blake, Norman. *Shakespeare's Language: An Introduction.* New York: St. Martin's Press, 1983.

This general introduction to Elizabethan English discusses various aspects of the language of Shakespeare and his contemporaries, offering possible meanings for hundreds of ambiguous constructions.

Dobson, E. J. *English Pronunciation, 1500–1700.* 2 vols. Oxford: Clarendon Press, 1968.

This long and technical work includes chapters on spelling (and its reformation), phonetics, stressed vowels, and consonants in early modern English.

Houston, John. *Shakespearean Sentences: A Study in Style and Syntax.* Baton Rouge: Louisiana State University Press, 1988.

Houston studies Shakespeare's stylistic choices, considering matters such as sentence length and the relative positions of subject, verb, and direct object. Examining plays throughout the canon in a roughly chronological, developmental order, he analyzes how sentence structure is used in setting tone, in characterization, and for other dramatic purposes.

Onions, C. T. *A Shakespeare Glossary.* Oxford: Clarendon Press, 1986.

This revised edition updates Onions's standard, selective glossary of words and phrases in Shakespeare's plays that are now obsolete, archaic, or obscure.

Partridge, Eric. *Shakespeare's Bawdy.* London: Routledge & Kegan Paul, 1955.
After an introductory essay, "The Sexual, the Homosexual, and Non-Sexual Bawdy in Shakespeare," Partridge provides a comprehensive glossary of "bawdy" phrases and words from the plays.

Robinson, Randal. *Unlocking Shakespeare's Language: Help for the Teacher and Student.* Urbana, Ill.: National Council of Teachers of English and the ERIC Clearinghouse on Reading and Communication Skills, 1989.
Specifically designed for the high-school and undergraduate college teacher and student, Robinson's book addresses the problems that most often hinder present-day readers of Shakespeare. Through work with his own students, Robinson found that many readers today are particularly puzzled by such stylistic devices as subject-verb inversion, interrupted structures, and compression. He shows how our own colloquial language contains comparable structures, and thus helps students recognize such structures when they find them in Shakespeare's plays. This book supplies worksheets—with examples from major plays—to illuminate and remedy such problems as unusual sequences of words and the separation of related parts of sentences.

Shakespeare's Life

Baldwin, T. W. *William Shakspere's Petty School.* Urbana: University of Illinois Press, 1943.
Baldwin here investigates the theory and practice of

the petty school, the first level of education in Elizabethan England. He focuses on that educational system primarily as it is reflected in Shakespeare's art.

Baldwin, T. W. *William Shakspere's Small Latine and Lesse Greeke.* 2 vols. Urbana: University of Illinois Press, 1944.

Baldwin attacks the view that Shakespeare was an uneducated genius—a view that had been dominant among Shakespeareans since the eighteenth century. Instead, Baldwin shows, the educational system of Shakespeare's time would have given the playwright a strong background in the classics, and there is much in the plays that shows how Shakespeare benefited from such an education.

Beier, A. L., and Roger Finlay, eds. *London 1500–1700: The Making of the Metropolis.* New York: Longman, 1986.

Focusing on the economic and social history of early modern London, these collected essays probe aspects of metropolitan life, including "Population and Disease," "Commerce and Manufacture," and "Society and Change."

Bentley, G. E. *Shakespeare's Life: A Biographical Handbook.* New Haven: Yale University Press, 1961.

This "just-the-facts" account presents the surviving documents of Shakespeare's life against an Elizabethan background.

Chambers, E. K. *William Shakespeare: A Study of Facts and Problems.* 2 vols. Oxford: Clarendon Press, 1930.

Analyzing in great detail the scant historical data, Chambers's complex, scholarly study considers the nature of the texts in which Shakespeare's work is preserved.

Cressy, David. *Education in Tudor and Stuart England.* London: Edward Arnold, 1975.

This volume collects sixteenth-, seventeenth-, and early-eighteenth-century documents detailing aspects of formal education in England, such as the curriculum, the control and organization of education, and the education of women.

Dutton, Richard. *William Shakespeare: A Literary Life.* New York: St. Martin's Press, 1989.

Not a biography in the traditional sense, Dutton's very readable work nevertheless "follows the contours of Shakespeare's life" as he examines Shakespeare's career as playwright and poet, with consideration of his patrons, theatrical associations, and audience.

Fraser, Russell. *Young Shakespeare.* New York: Columbia University Press, 1988.

Fraser focuses on Shakespeare's first thirty years, paying attention simultaneously to his life and art.

De Grazia, Margreta. *Shakespeare Verbatim: The Reproduction of Authenticity and the Apparatus of 1790.* Oxford: Clarendon Press, 1991.

De Grazia traces and discusses the development of such editorial criteria as authenticity, historical periodization, factual biography, chronological development, and close reading, locating as the point of origin Edmond Malone's 1790 edition of Shakespeare's works. There are interesting chapters on the First Folio and on the "legendary" versus the "documented" Shakespeare.

Schoenbaum, S. *William Shakespeare: A Compact Documentary Life.* New York: Oxford University Press, 1977.

This standard biography economically presents the

essential documents from Shakespeare's time in an accessible narrative account of the playwright's life.

Shakespeare's Theater

Bentley, G. E. *The Profession of Player in Shakespeare's Time, 1590–1642.* Princeton: Princeton University Press, 1984.

Bentley readably sets forth a wealth of evidence about performance in Shakespeare's time, with special attention to the relations between player and company, and the business of casting, managing, and touring.

Berry, Herbert. *Shakespeare's Playhouses.* New York: AMS Press, 1987.

Berry's six essays collected here discuss (with illustrations) varying aspects of the four playhouses in which Shakespeare had a financial stake: the Theatre in Shoreditch, the Blackfriars, and the first and second Globe.

Cook, Ann Jennalie. *The Privileged Playgoers of Shakespeare's London.* Princeton: Princeton University Press, 1981.

Cook's work argues, on the basis of sociological, economic, and documentary evidence, that Shakespeare's audience—and the audience for English Renaissance drama generally—consisted mainly of the "privileged."

Greg, W. W. *Dramatic Documents from the Elizabethan Playhouses.* 2 vols. Oxford: Clarendon Press, 1931.

Greg itemizes and briefly describes almost all the play manuscripts that survive from the period 1590 to around 1660, including, among other things, players' parts. His second volume offers facsimiles of selected manuscripts.

Gurr, Andrew. *Playgoing in Shakespeare's London.* Cambridge: Cambridge University Press, 1987.
     Gurr charts how the theatrical enterprise developed from its modest beginnings in the late 1560s to become a thriving institution in the 1600s. He argues that there were important changes over the period 1567–1644 in the playhouses, the audience, and the plays.

Harbage, Alfred. *Shakespeare's Audience.* New York: Columbia University Press, 1941.
     Harbage investigates the fragmentary surviving evidence to interpret the size, composition, and behavior of Shakespeare's audience.

Hattaway, Michael. *Elizabethan Popular Theatre: Plays in Performance.* London: Routledge & Kegan Paul, 1982.
     Beginning with a study of the popular drama of the late Elizabethan age—a description of the stages, performance conditions, and acting of the period—this volume concludes with an analysis of five well-known plays of the 1590s, one of them (*Titus Andronicus*) by Shakespeare.

Shapiro, Michael. *Children of the Revels: The Boy Companies of Shakespeare's Time and Their Plays.* New York: Columbia University Press, 1977.
     Shapiro chronicles the history of the amateur and quasi-professional child companies that flourished in London at the end of Elizabeth's reign and the beginning of James's.

The Publication of Shakespeare's Plays

Blayney, Peter. *The First Folio of Shakespeare*. Hanover, Md.: Folger, 1991.

Blayney's accessible account of the printing and later life of the First Folio—an amply illustrated catalog to a 1991 Folger Shakespeare Library exhibition—analyzes the mechanical production of the First Folio, describing how the Folio was made, by whom and for whom, how much it cost, and its ups and downs (or, rather, downs and ups) since its printing in 1623.

Hinman, Charlton. *The Printing and Proof-Reading of the First Folio of Shakespeare*. 2 vols. Oxford: Clarendon Press, 1963.

In the most arduous study of a single book ever undertaken, Hinman attempts to reconstruct how the Shakespeare First Folio of 1623 was set into type and run off the press, sheet by sheet. He also provides almost all the known variations in readings from copy to copy.

Hinman, Charlton. *The Norton Facsimile: The First Folio of Shakespeare*. New York: W. W. Norton, 1968.

This facsimile presents a photographic reproduction of an "ideal" copy of the First Folio of Shakespeare; Hinman attempts to represent each page in its most fully corrected state.

Key to
Famous Lines and Phrases

He hath indeed better bettered expectation than you
must expect of me to tell you how.
                                   [*Messenger*—1.1.15–17]

How much better is it to weep at joy than to joy at
weeping!   [*Leonato*—1.1.27–29]

He is a very valiant trencherman . . .
                                         [*Beatrice*—1.1.50]

. . . the gentleman is not in your books.
                                [*Messenger*—1.1.76–77]

". . . Benedick the married man." [*Benedick*—1.1.262]

. . . as merry as the day is long.   [*Beatrice*—2.1.49]

Speak low if you speak love.   [*Prince*—2.1.97]

. . . it keeps on the windy side of care.
                                  [*Beatrice*—2.1.307–8]

I was born to speak all mirth and no matter.
                              [*Beatrice*—2.1.322–23]

. . . I will tell you my drift.   [*Prince*—2.1.378]

He was wont to speak plain and to the purpose . . .
                              [*Benedick*—2.3.18–19]

He hath a heart as sound as a bell . . .
[*Prince*—3.2.11–12]

Are you good men and true?   [*Dogberry*—3.3.1]

. . . you may say they are not the men you took them
for.   [*Dogberry*—3.3.46–47]

. . . they that touch pitch will be defiled.
[*Dogberry*—3.3.56]

Not for the wide world.   [*Benedick*—4.1.304]

. . . there was never yet philosopher
That could endure the toothache patiently . . .
[*Leonato*—5.1.37–38]

. . . some of us will smart for it.
[*Leonato's Brother*—5.1.122]

What though care killed a cat? Thou hast mettle
enough in thee to kill care.   [*Claudio*—5.1.145–47]

. . . I was not born under a rhyming planet . . .
[*Benedick*—5.2.40–41]